Math in Focus®

Singapore Math®
by Marshall Cavendish®

GRADE
KB

Student Book
Part 1

Author
Dr. Pamela Sharpe

U.S. Consultants
Andy Clark
Patsy F. Kanter

Marshall Cavendish Education

U.S. Distributor
Houghton
Mifflin
Harcourt

Published by Marshall Cavendish Education
Times Centre, 1 New Industrial Road, Singapore 536196
Customer Service Hotline: (65) 6213 9688
US Office Tel: (1-914) 332 8888 | Fax: (1-914) 332 8882
E-mail: cs@mceducation.com
Website: www.mceducation.com

Distributed by
Houghton Mifflin Harcourt
222 Berkeley Street
Boston, MA 02116
Tel: 617-351-5000
Website: www.hmheducation.com/mathinfocus

Cover: © Bob Elsdale/Eureka/Alamy.
Image provided by Houghton Mifflin Harcourt.

First published 2018

ISBN 978-1-328-88059-8

Printed in Singapore

9 10 11 12 1401 24 23 22 21
4500833961 A B C D E

Contents

Contents

Chapter 7 Solid and Flat Shapes

Lesson 1 Solid Shapes

Which shape is it? Color.

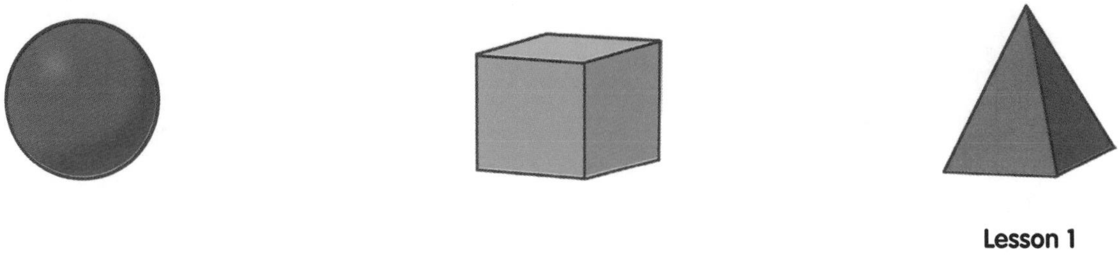

Match.

Pair.

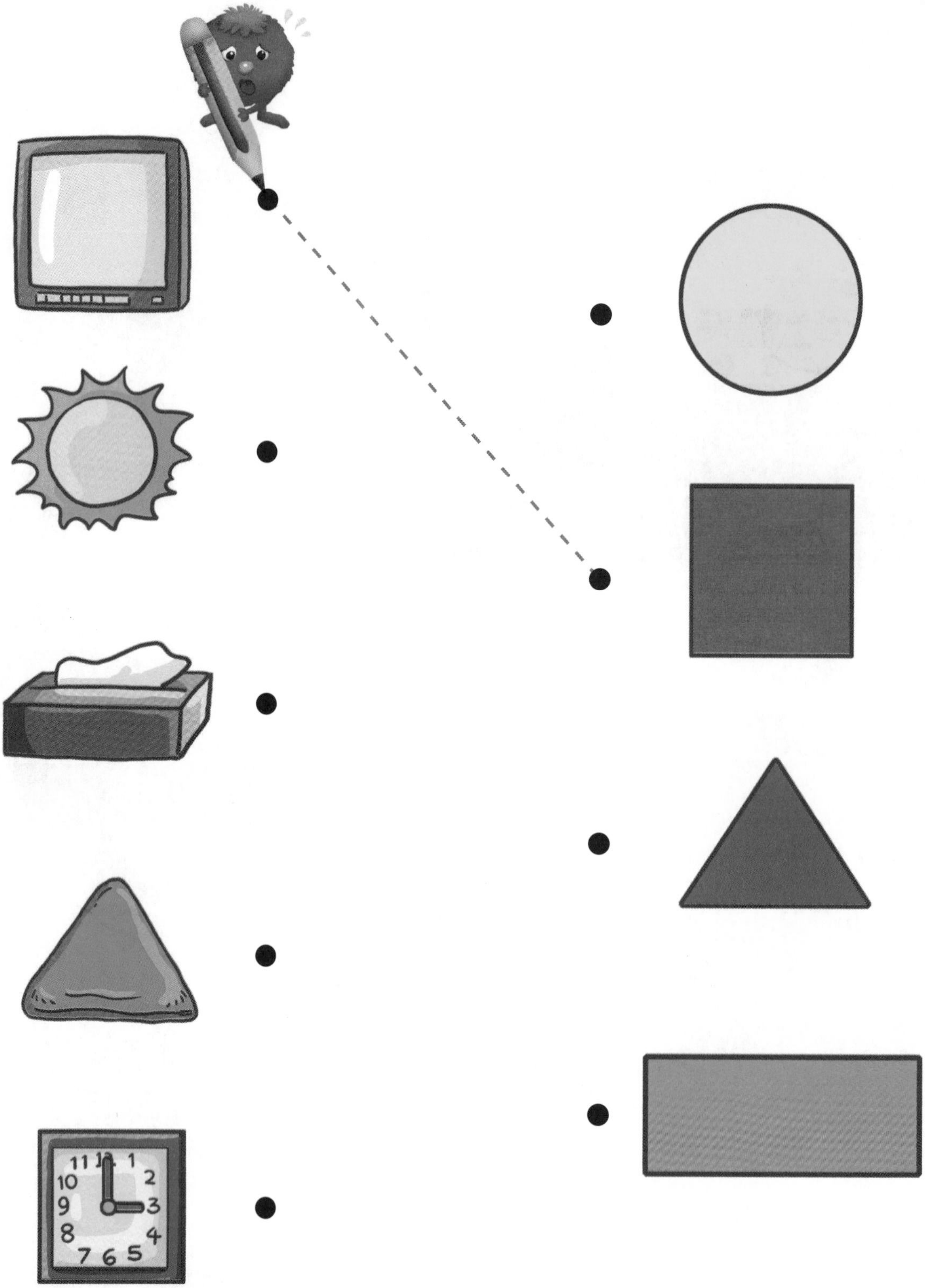

Lesson 3 Flat Shapes

Draw.

1

Big circle

Small circle

2

Small square

Big square

3

Big triangle

Small triangle

4

Small rectangle

Big rectangle

5

Big hexagon

Small hexagon

Lesson 4 **Flat Shape Pictures**

Color the squares red. Color the rectangles green. Color the circles yellow. Color the triangles blue. Color the hexagons brown.

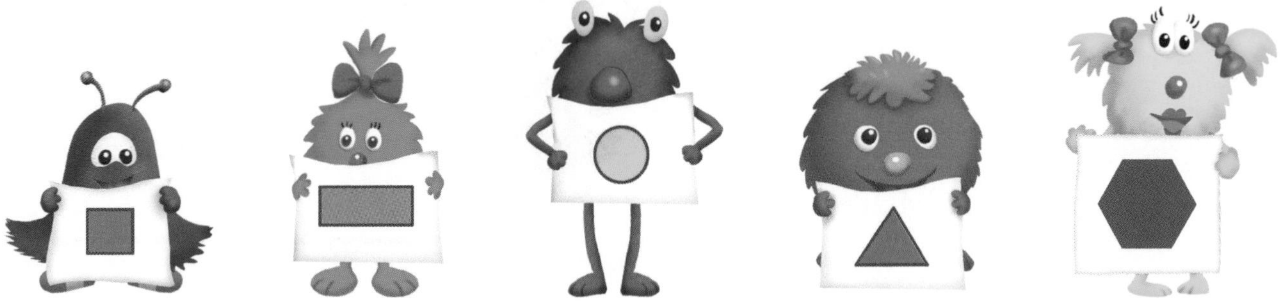

Lesson 5 Shape Patterns

Complete the pattern.

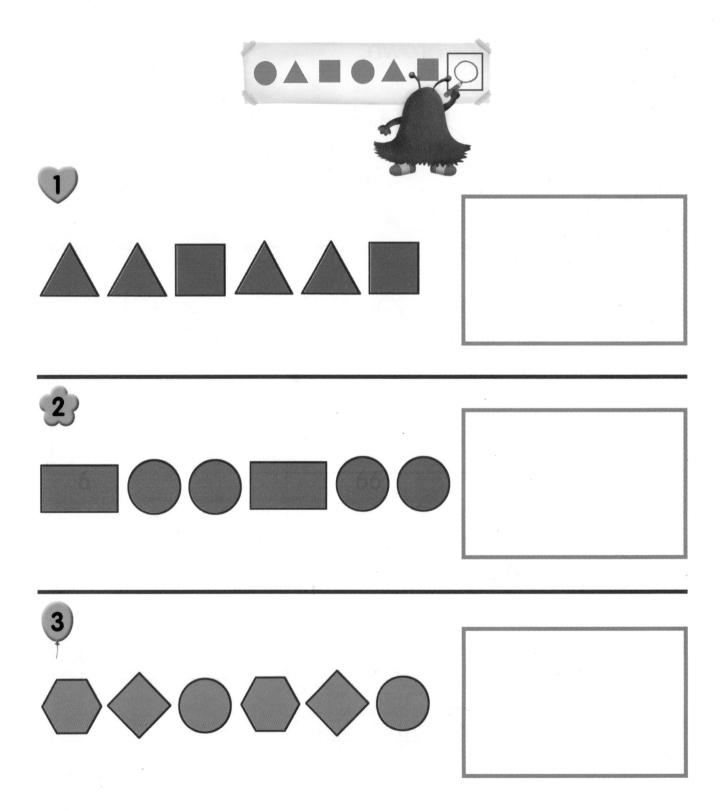

1

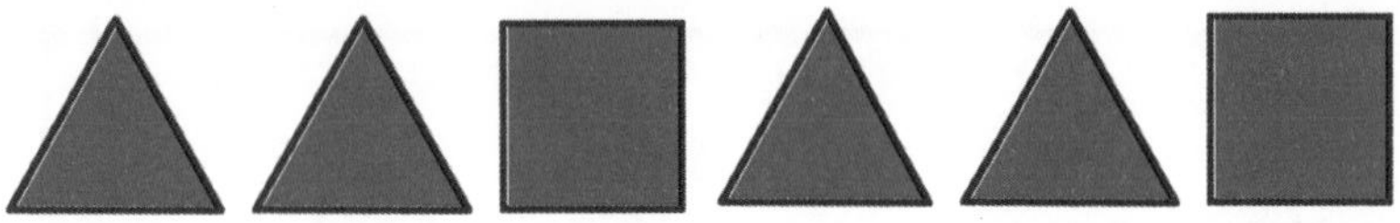

2

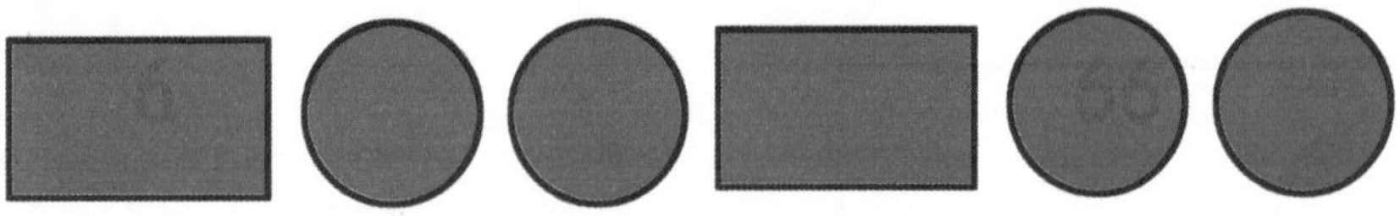

3

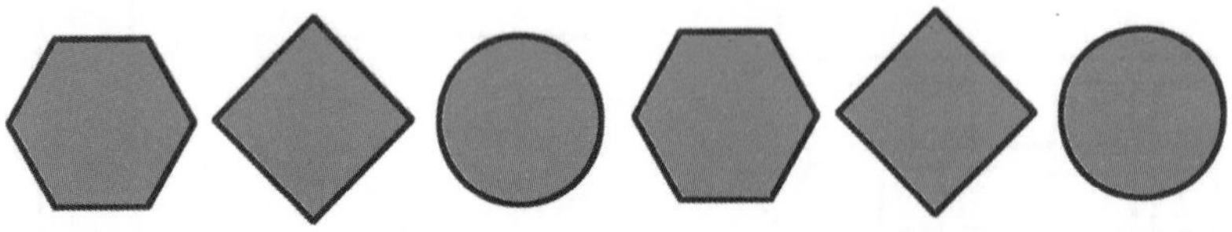

Chapter 8

Numbers to 100

Lesson 1 Counting by 2s

Count and write.

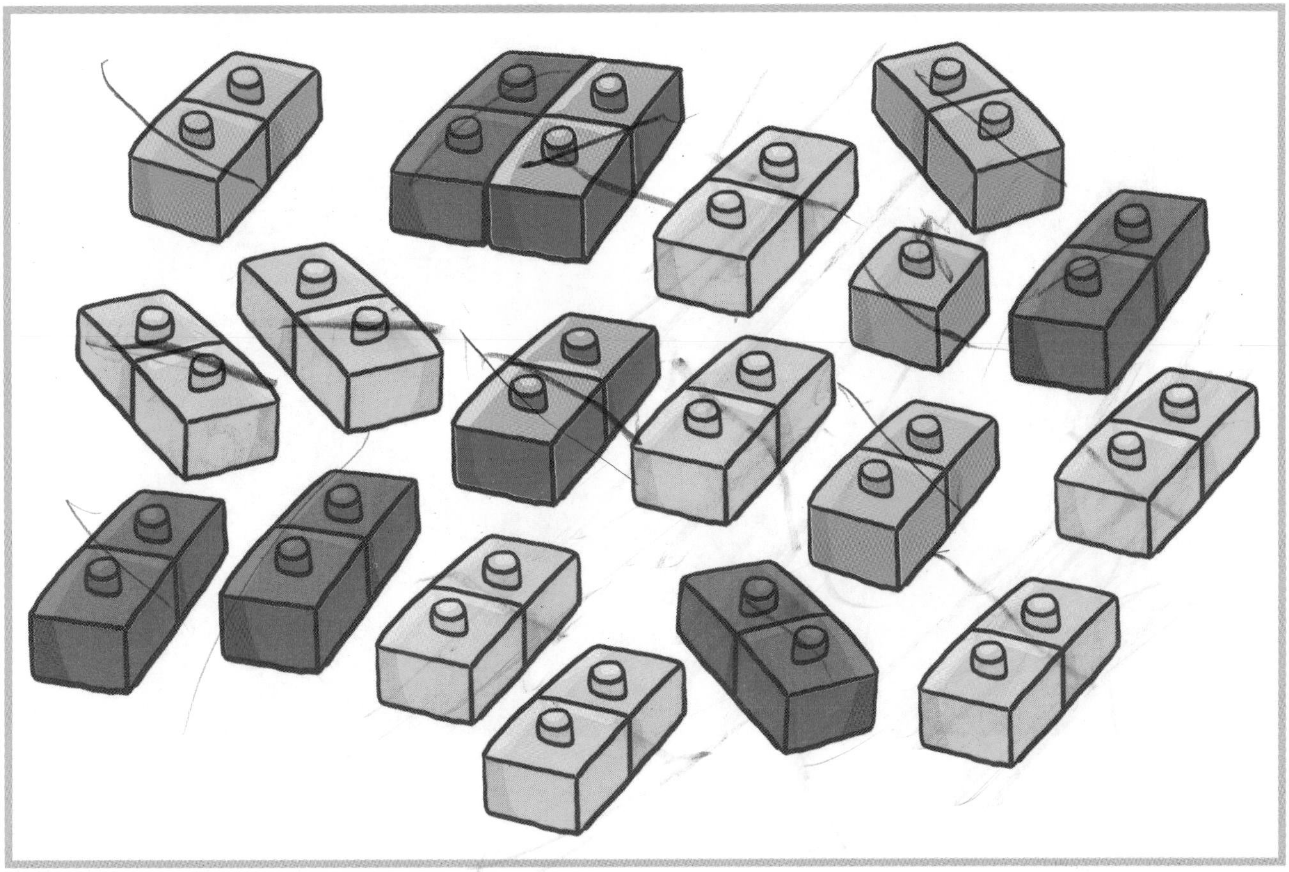

 16

 10

 7

 4

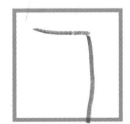

Lesson 2 Counting by 5s

Circle the groups of 5 ants.

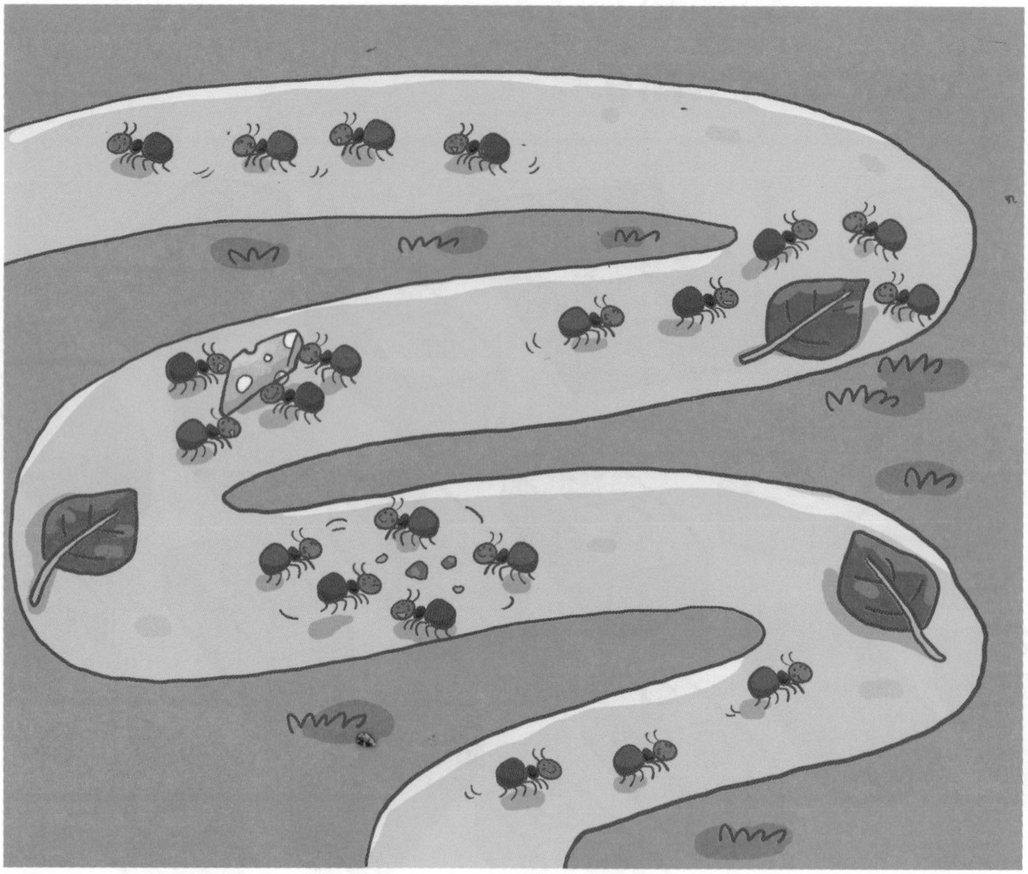

Make the tally.

 Counting by 10s to 100

How many? Count and circle.

1

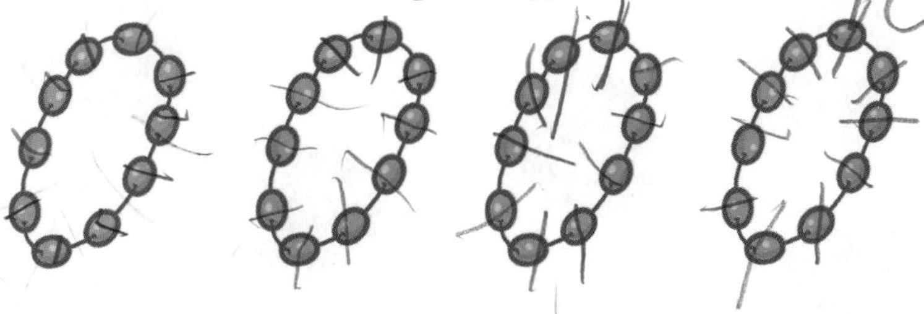

40 14 50

2

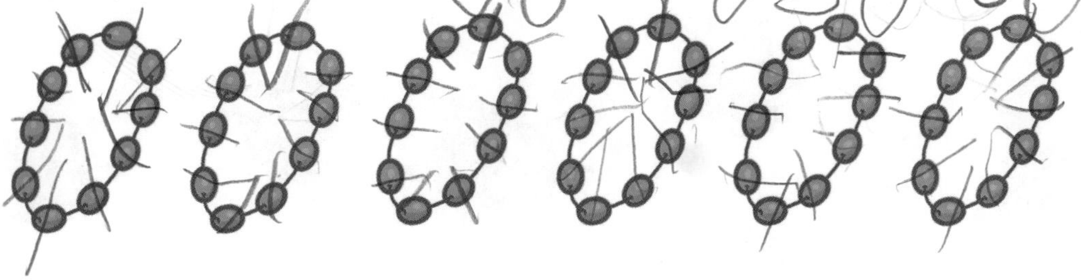

16 80 60

3

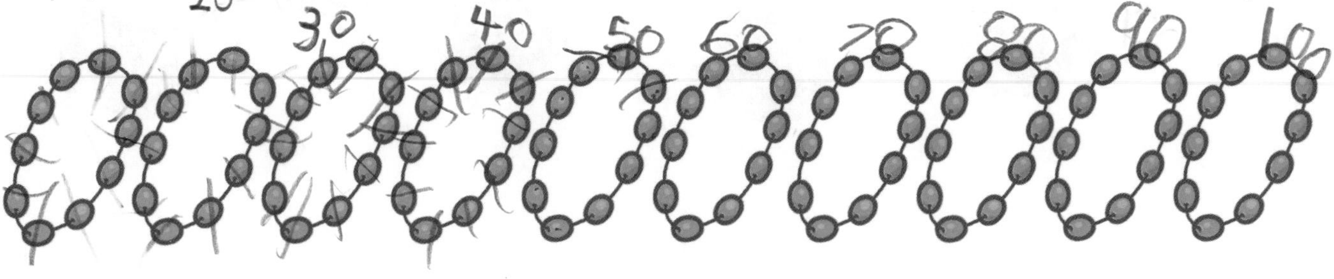

11 100 90

Circle groups of 10. Then, count and circle.

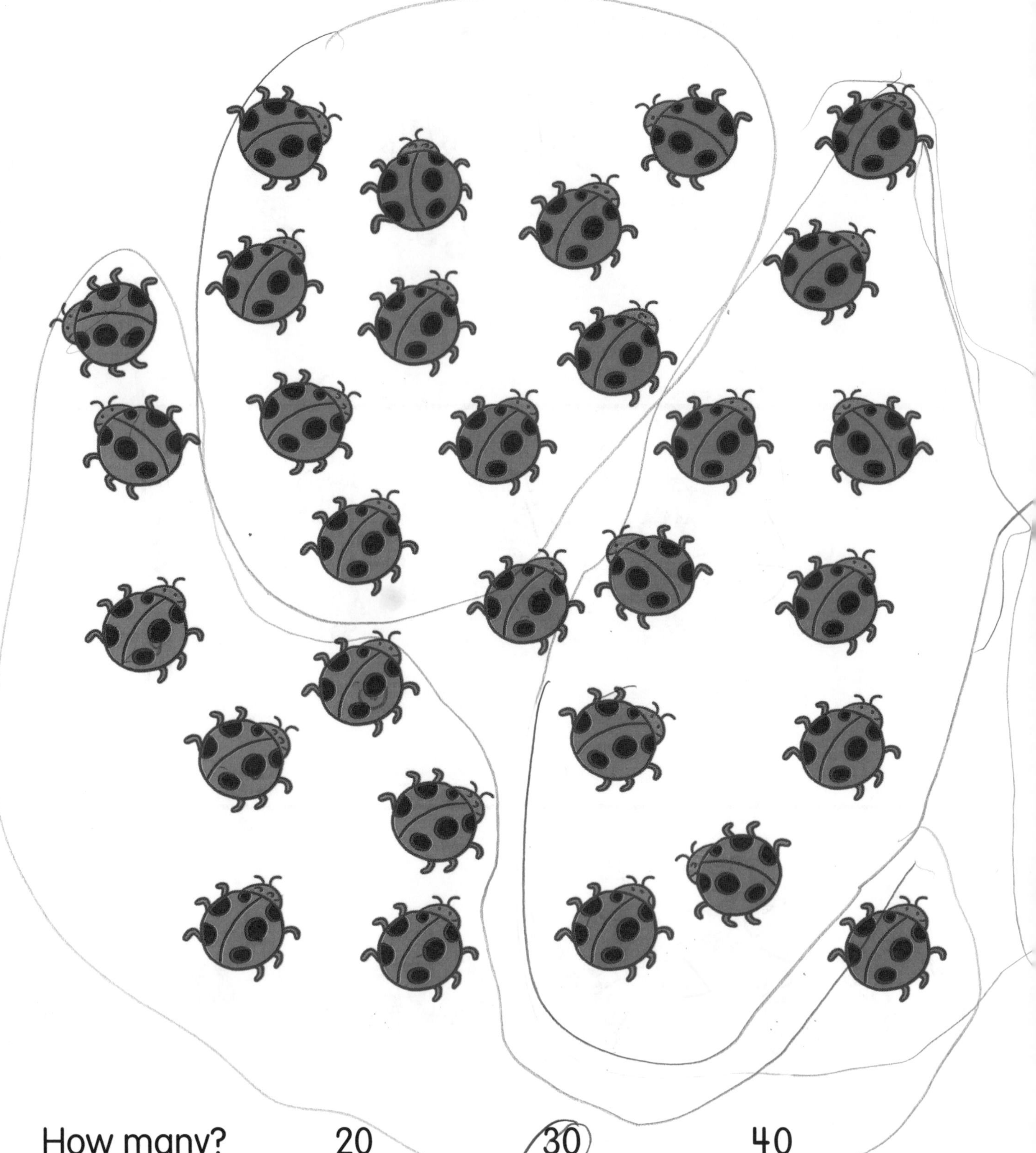

How many? 20 30 40

Lesson 4 Numbers 20 to 49

Read and color.

1

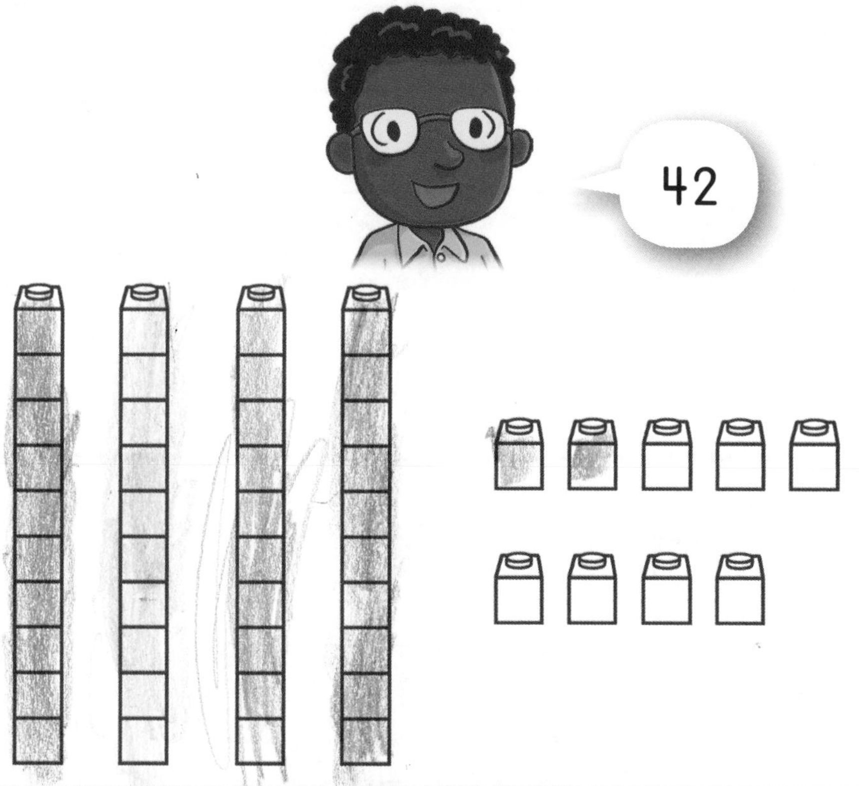

2

How many? Count and circle.

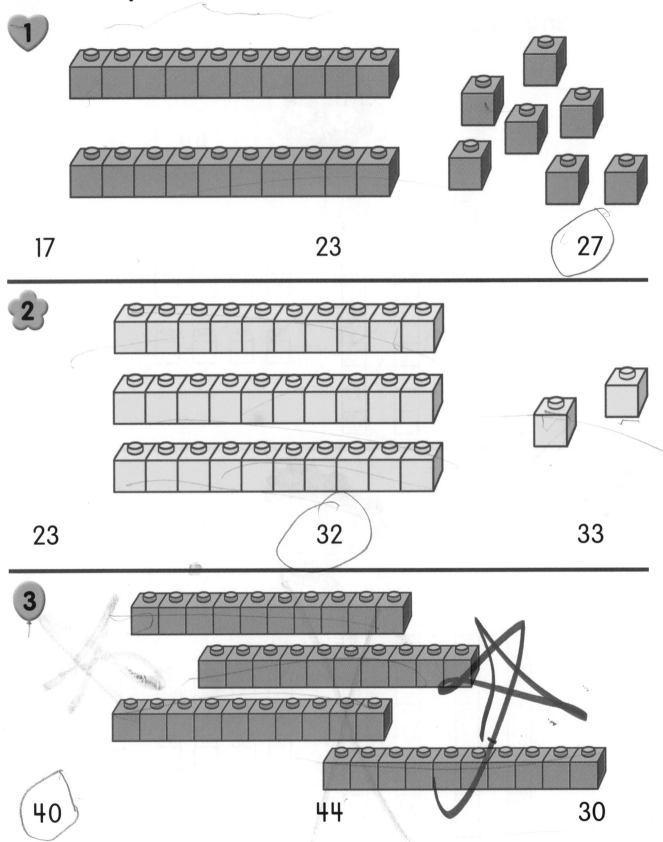

1

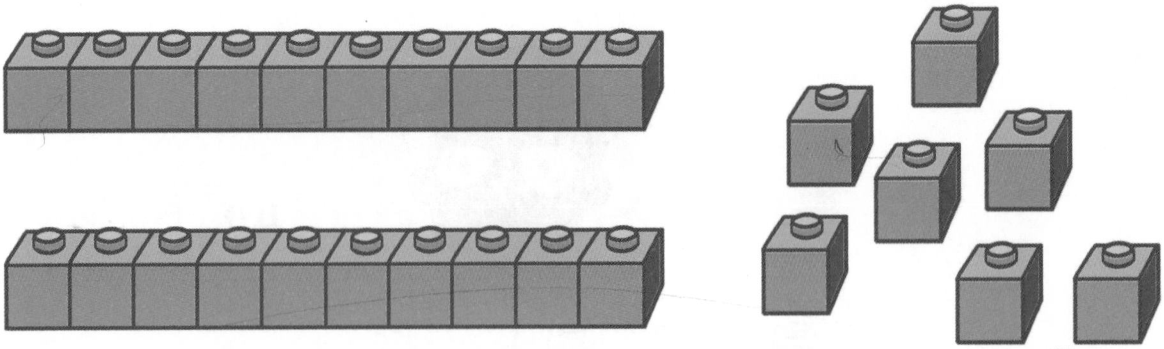

17 23 27

2

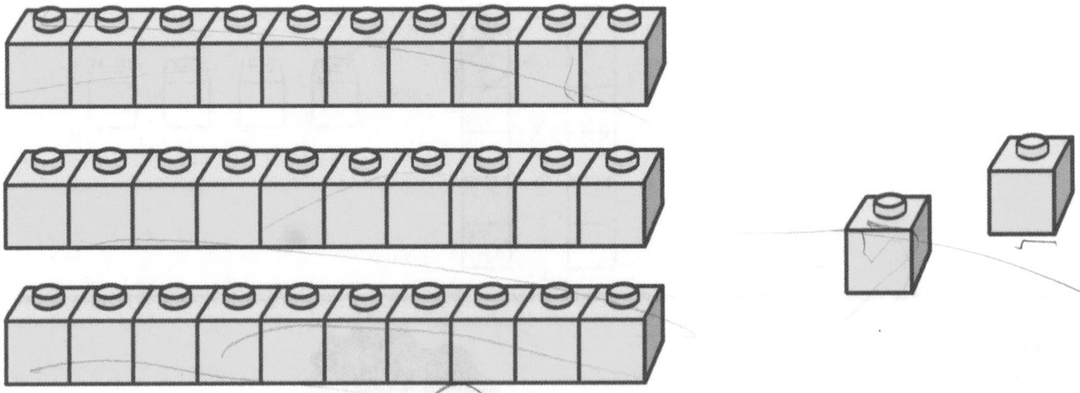

23 32 33

3

40 44 30

Complete the sequence. Circle the missing number.

1

20, 21, ___, 23

24 22 32

2

39, ___, 41, 42

38 30 40

3

27, 28, 29, ___

26 40 30

Lesson 5 Numbers 50 to 79

How many? Count and circle.

1

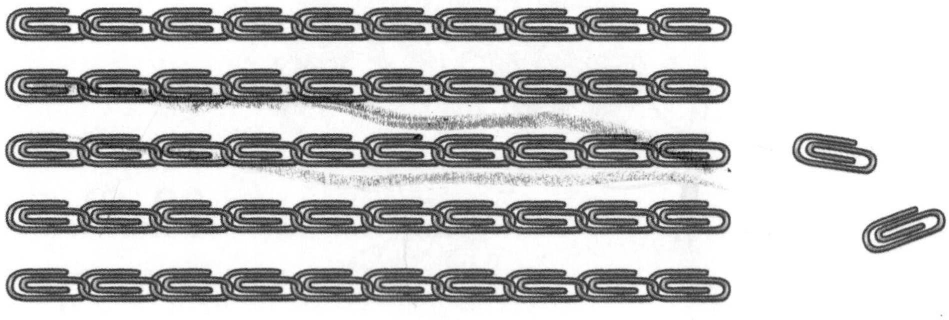

25 50 52

2

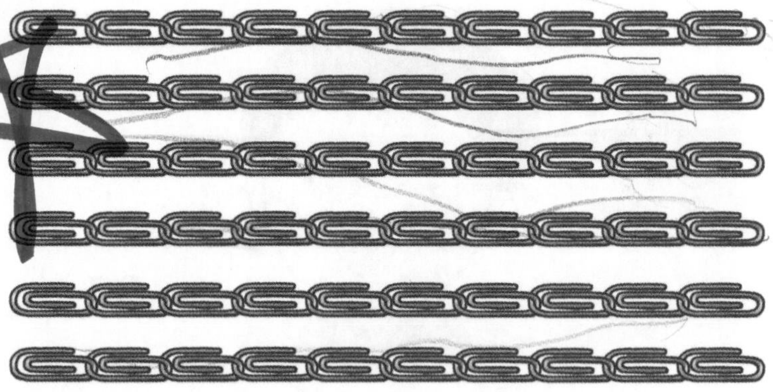

6 66 60

3

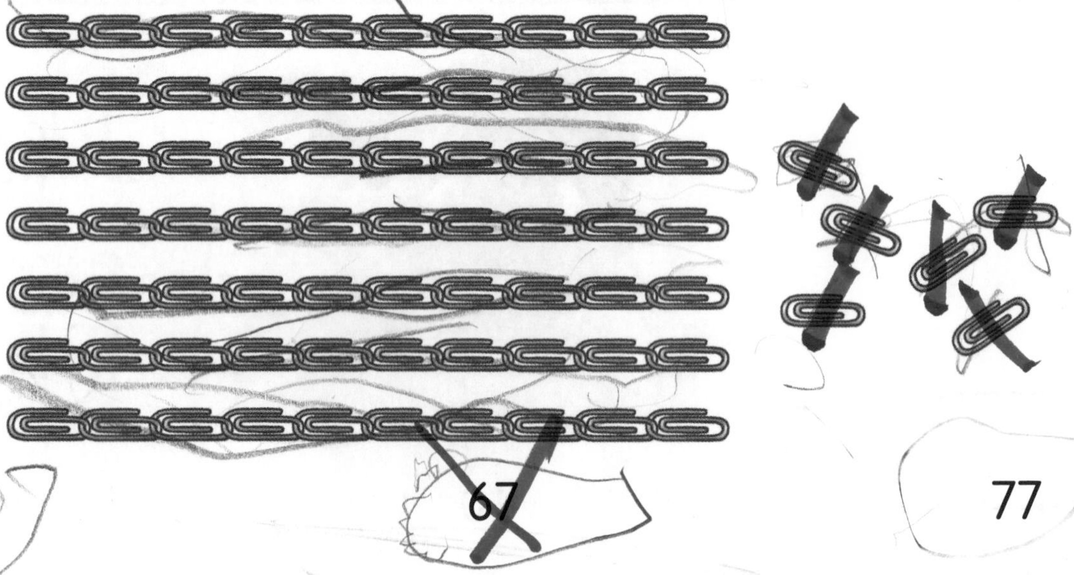

76 67 77

Which is the missing number? Color the balloon.

1

2

3

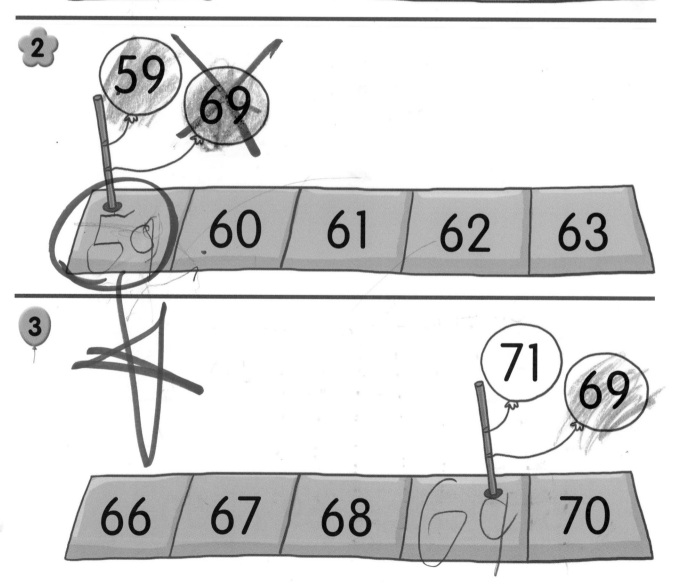

Color the least number orange.
Color the greatest number blue.

1

69	72	77	67

2

52	57	51	50

3

79	73	70	60

4

51	78	69	50	71

How many? Count and circle.

1

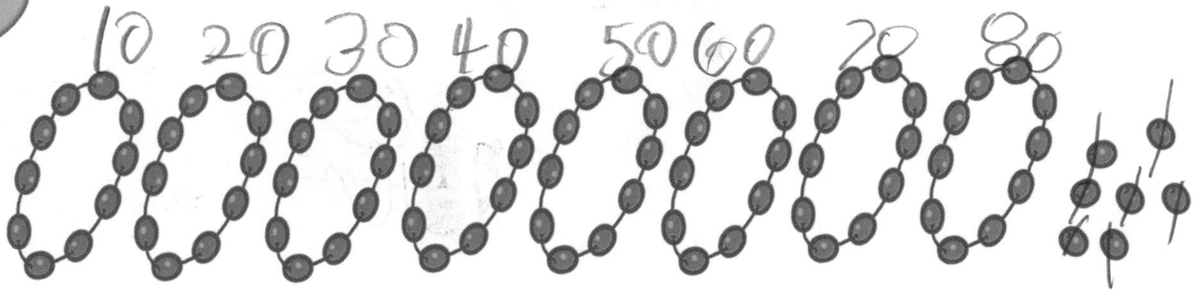

78 87 88

2

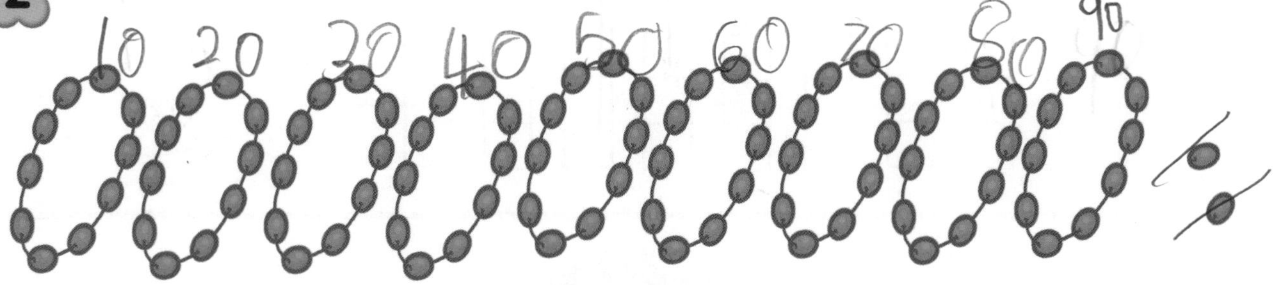

90 29 92

3

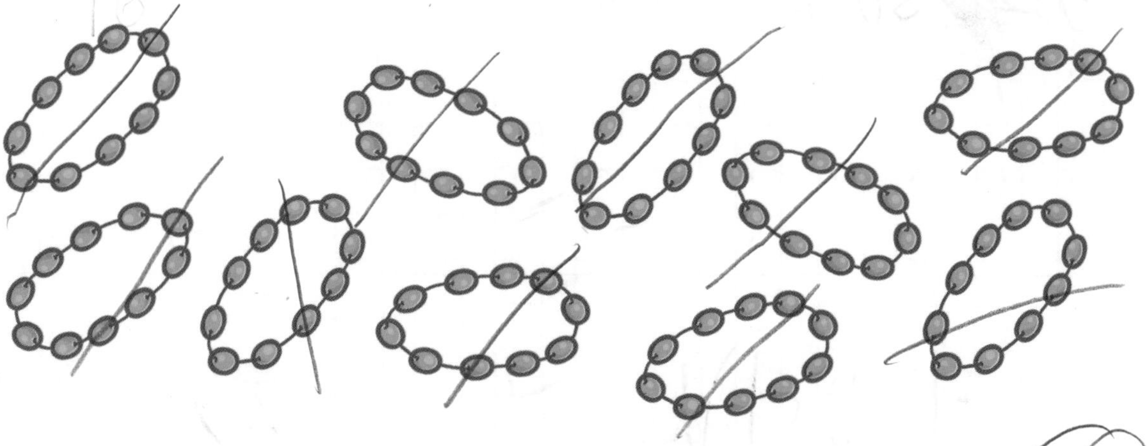

80 90 100

Read and color.

1

2

Which is the missing number? Color the flag.

1

2

3

Lesson 7 Numbers 1 to 100

What comes before? Color blue.
What comes after? Color red.

1

5	49	52	51

2

10	21	12	1

3

79	100	89	98

Chapter 9 Comparing Sets

Lesson 1 Comparing Sets of Up to 10

Count and write.

1

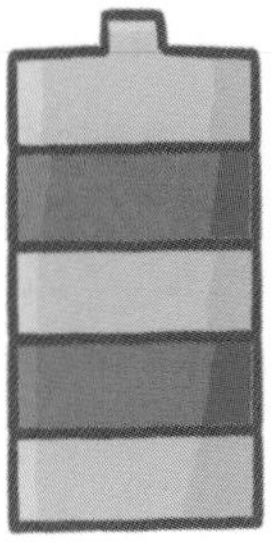

2

3

4

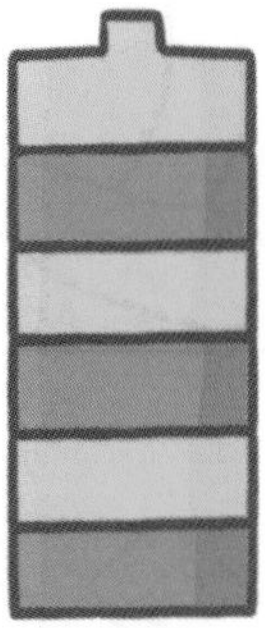

Which has more? Color.
Which has fewer? Circle.

1

2

3

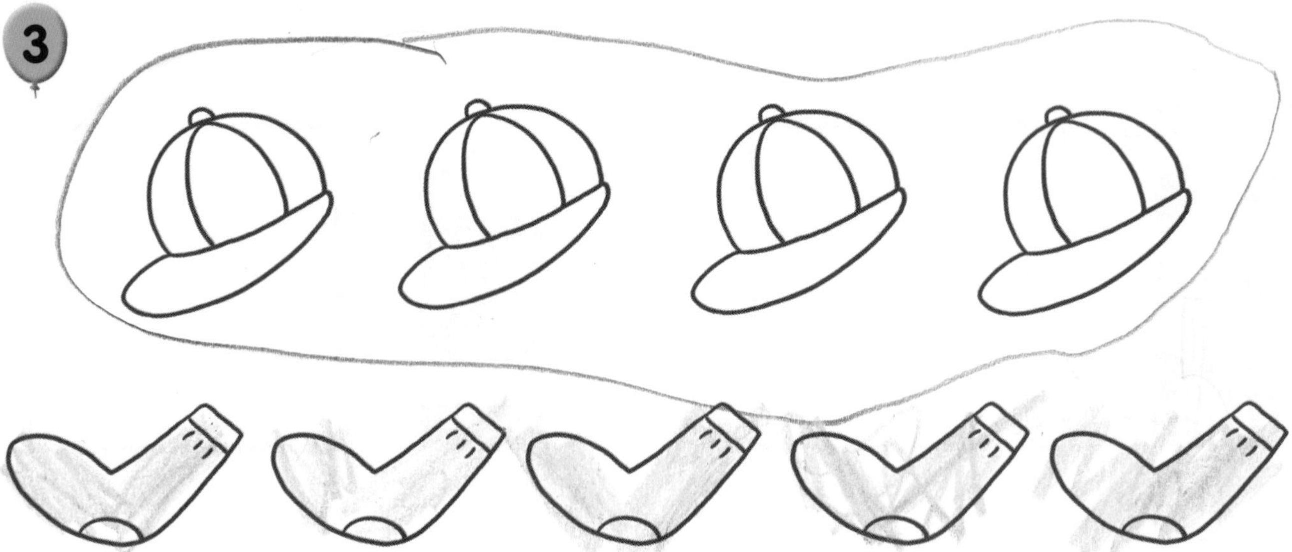

What cannot be counted? Circle.

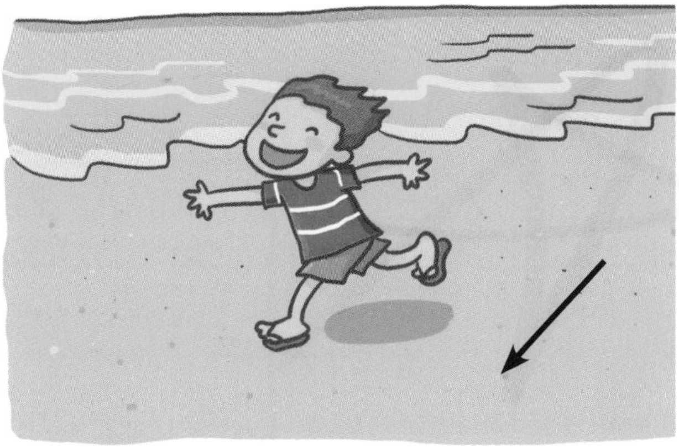

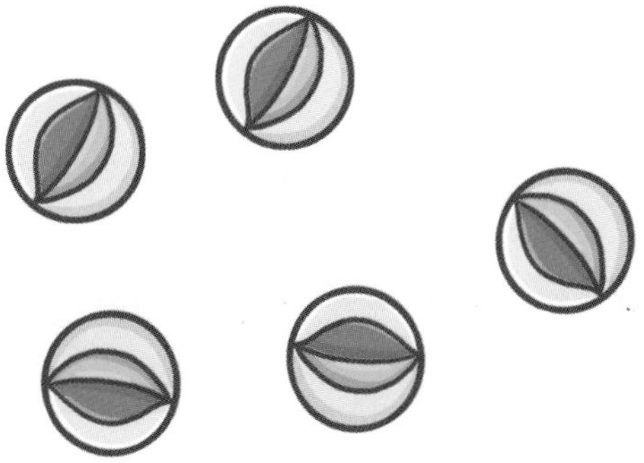

Lesson 2 Comparing Sets of 11 to 20

Count and write.
Circle the set with more.

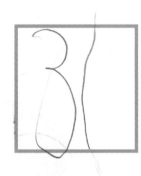

1

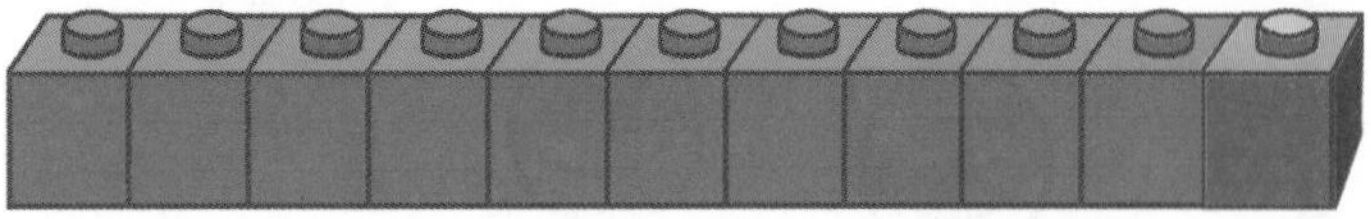

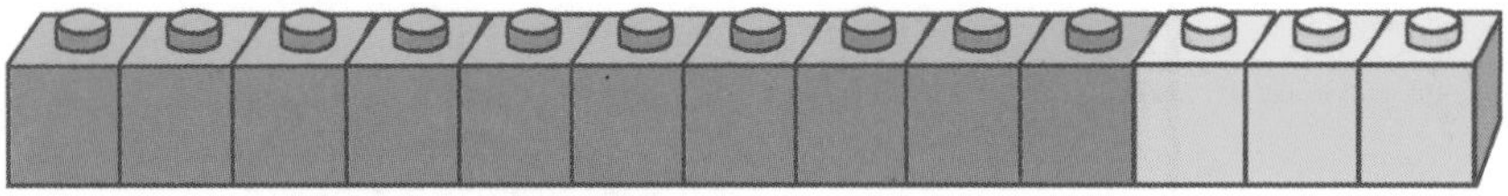

2

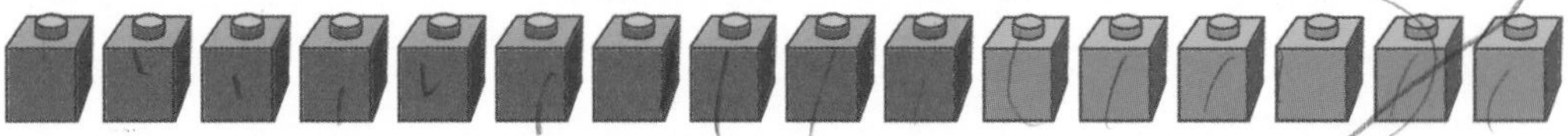

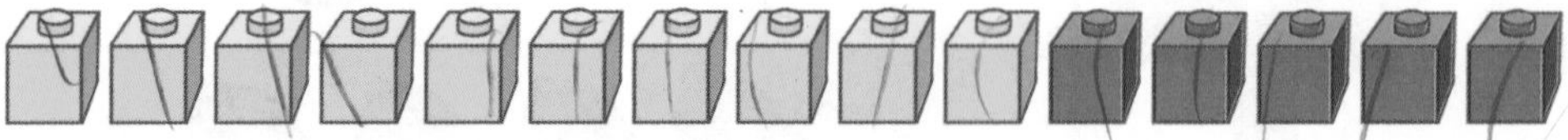

Match one-to-one.
Then, color the set with fewer.

1

2

3

Lesson 3 Comparing Sets to Find the Difference

Color the extra cubes red.
Count and write how many more.

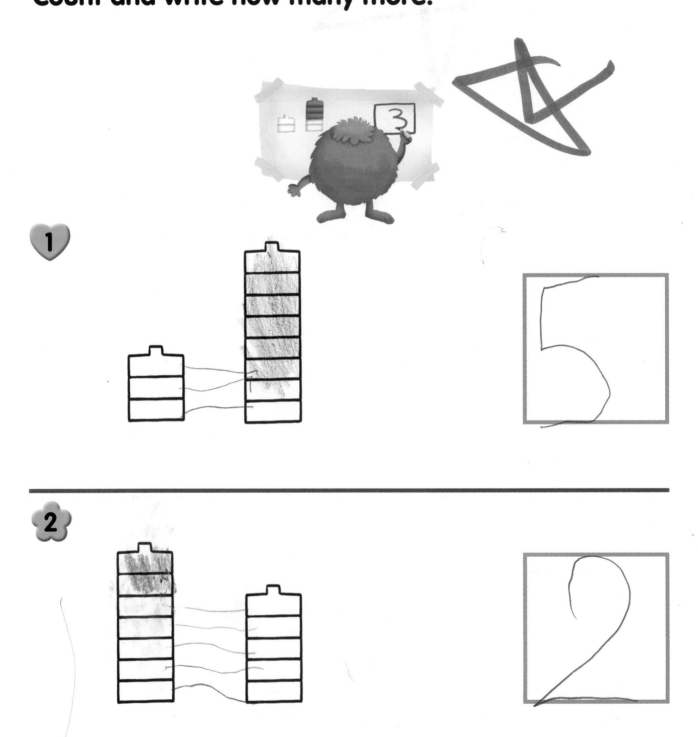

1

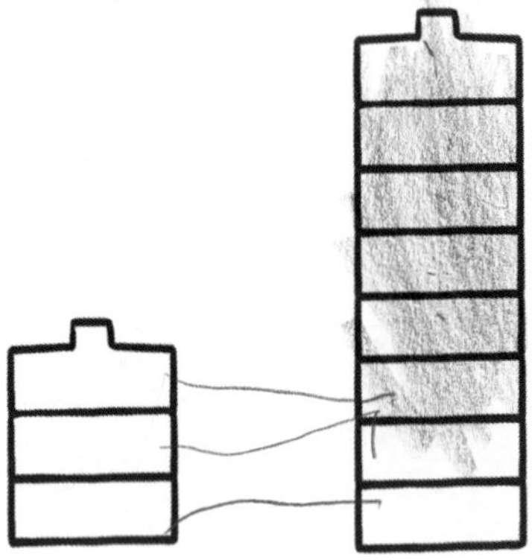

2

3

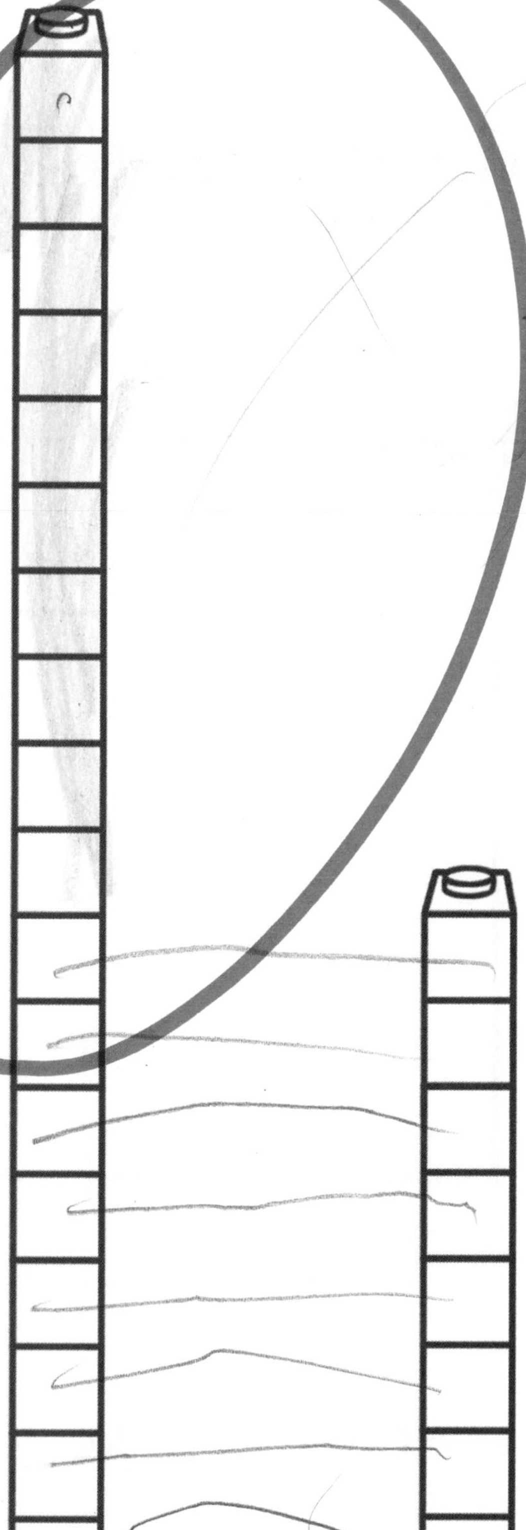

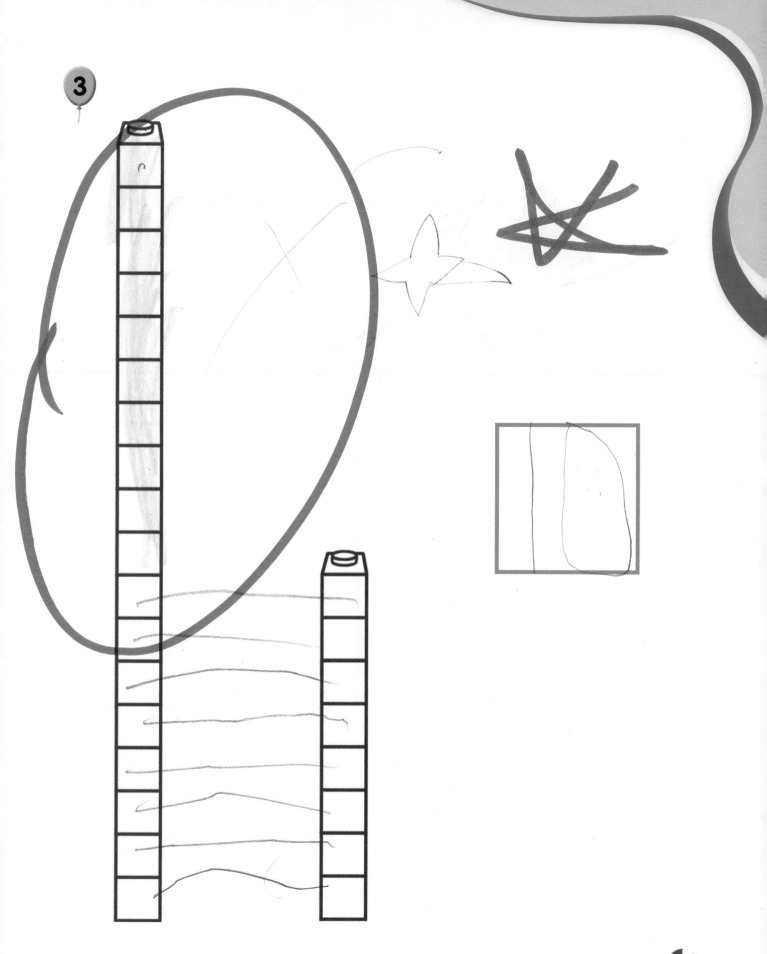

Draw, count, and write.

1

Draw a tower of 3 cubes in Box A.

Draw a tower of 5 cubes in Box B.

Box A

Box B

The tower in Box A has ______ fewer cubes than the tower in Box B.

2

Draw 14 cubes in Box C.

Draw 11 cubes in Box D.

Box C	Box D

Box C has _____ more cubes than Box D.

Lesson 4 Combining Sets

Count and circle.

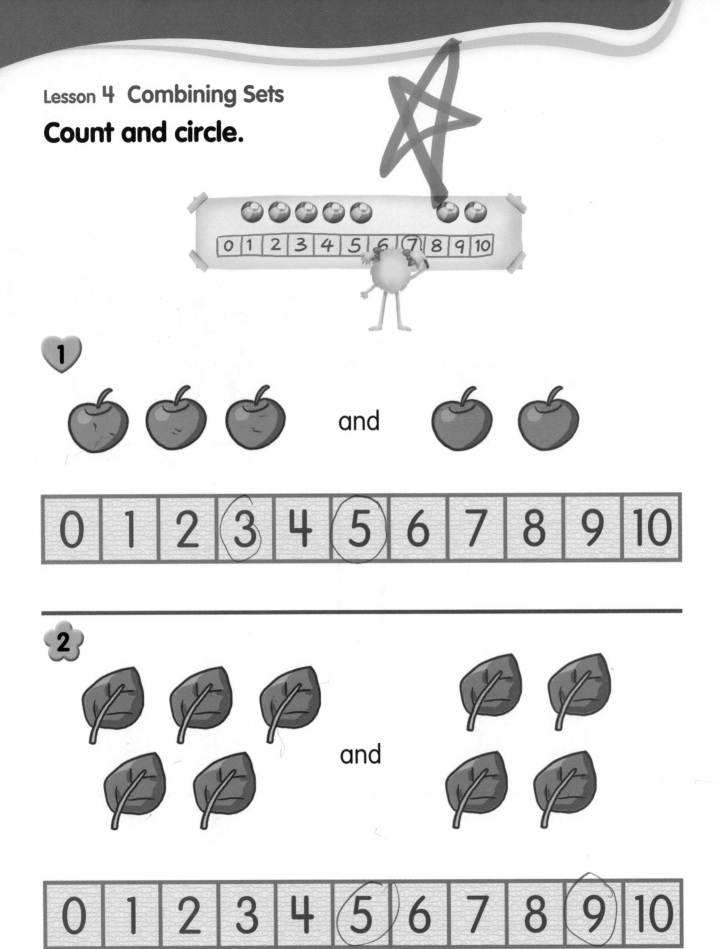

1

0	1	2	3	4	5	6	7	8	9	10

2

0	1	2	3	4	5	6	7	8	9	10

3

and

0	1	2	3	4	5	6	7	8	9	10	11	12	13	14	15	16	17	18	19	20

4

and

0	1	2	3	4	5	6	7	8	9	10	11	12	13	14	15	16	17	18	19	20

5

and

0	1	2	3	4	5	6	7	8	9	10	11	12	13	14	15	16	17	18	19	20

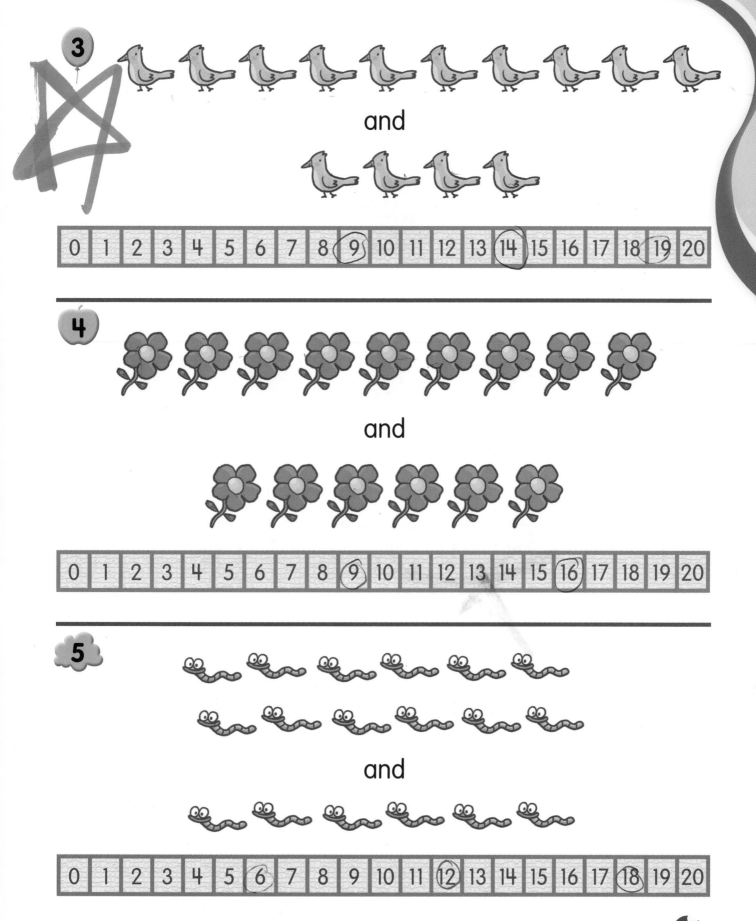

Count, circle, and write.

1

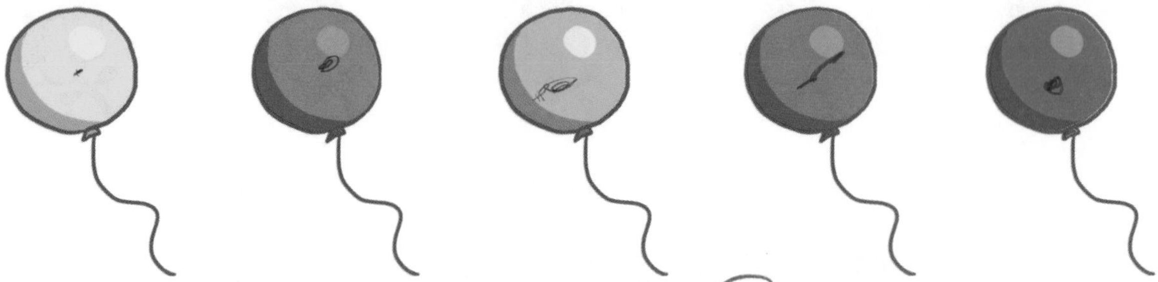

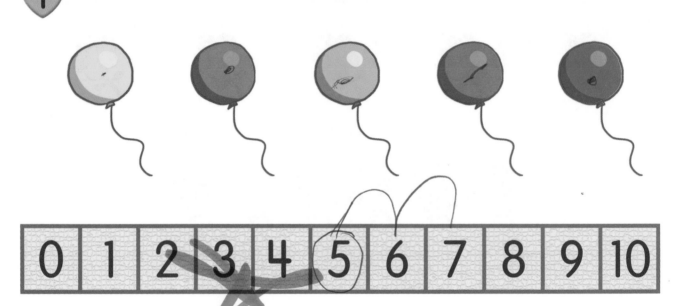

0	1	2	3	4	5	6	7	8	9	10

If I add 2 more balloons, there will be 7 balloons altogether.

2

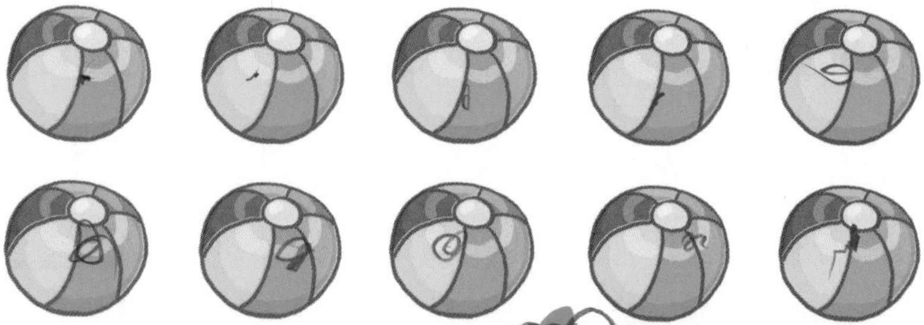

0	1	2	3	4	5	6	7	8	9	10	11	12	13	14	15	16	17	18	19	20

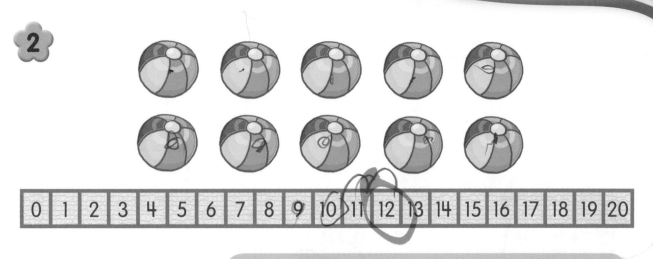

If I add 2 more balls, there will be [12] balls altogether.

3

0	1	2	3	4	5	6	7	8	9	10	11	12	13	14	15	16	17	18	19	20

If I add 5 more cups, there will be [15] cups altogether.

Count and write.

1

and

is 3

2

and

is 7

3

and

is 7

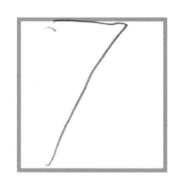

4

and

is

5

and

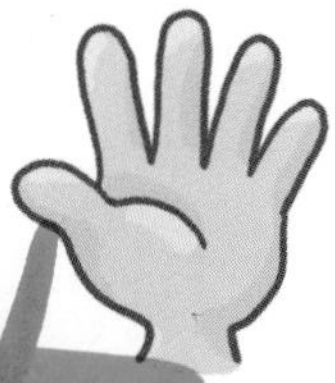

is

6

and

is

Chapter 10 Ordinal Numbers

Lesson 1 Sequencing Events

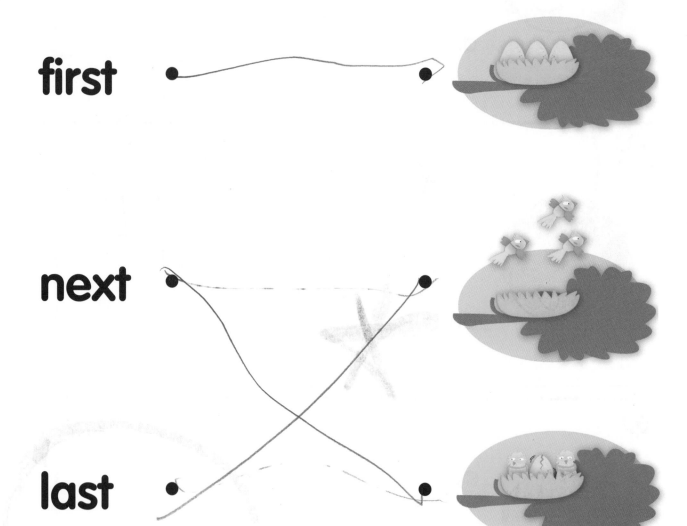

Pair.

first 

next 

last 

Color the frames.

first

next

last

Color.

first	second
third	last

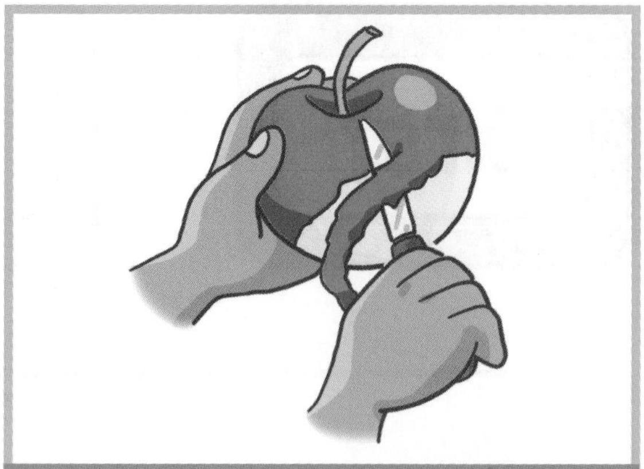

first	second
third	last

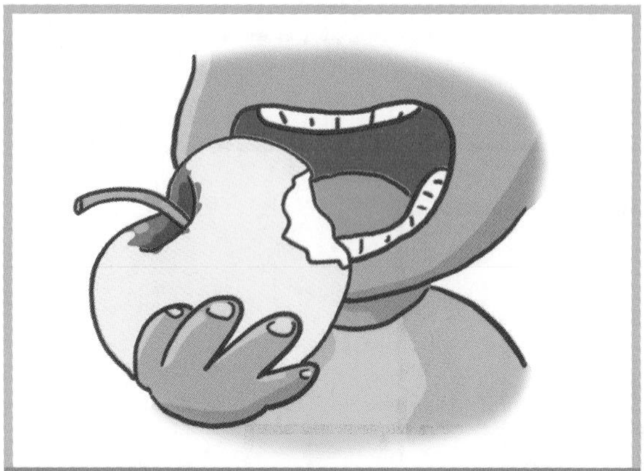

first	second
third	last

first	second
third	last

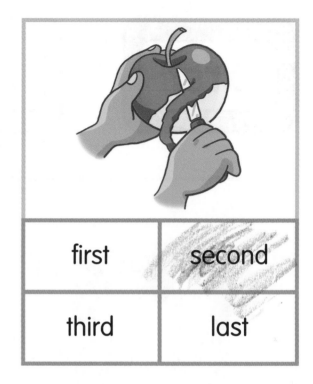

Color the child that comes before Baby Bear.
Circle the child that comes after Baby Bear.

Lesson 3 Showing Your Preferences

Pair.

1st choice • •

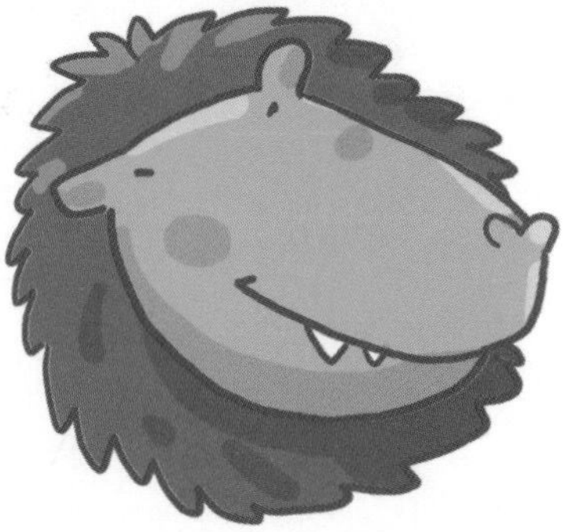

2nd choice • •

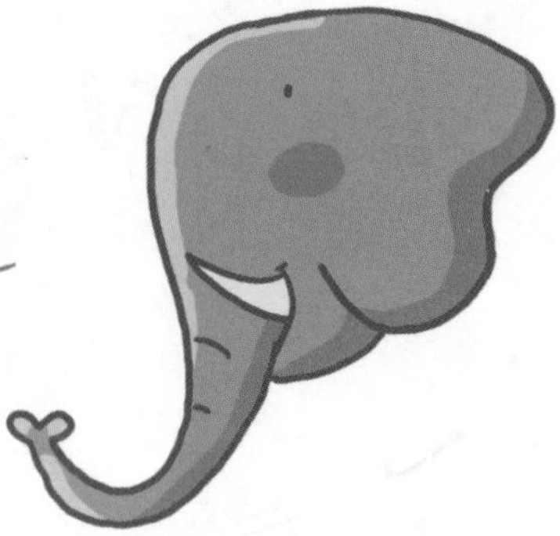

3rd choice • •

Chapter 11 Calendar Patterns

Lesson 1 Days of the Week

What day is it today? Color green.
What day was it yesterday? Color blue.
What day will it be tomorrow? Color yellow.

Sunday	Monday	
Tuesday	Wednesday	Thursday
Friday	Saturday	

Read and circle.

This day comes after Saturday and before Monday. Which day is it?

Saturday **Sunday** **Monday** **Tuesday**

Lesson 2 Months of the Year

Make an X on the month before August. Circle the month after February. Color the month between October and December.

January	February	March
April	May	June
July	August	September
October	November	December

Chapter 12

Counting On and Counting Back

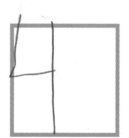

Lesson 1 Counting On to 10

How many more to make 10? Count and write.

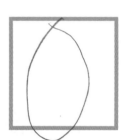

1

2

3

4

How many more to make 10? Count and write.

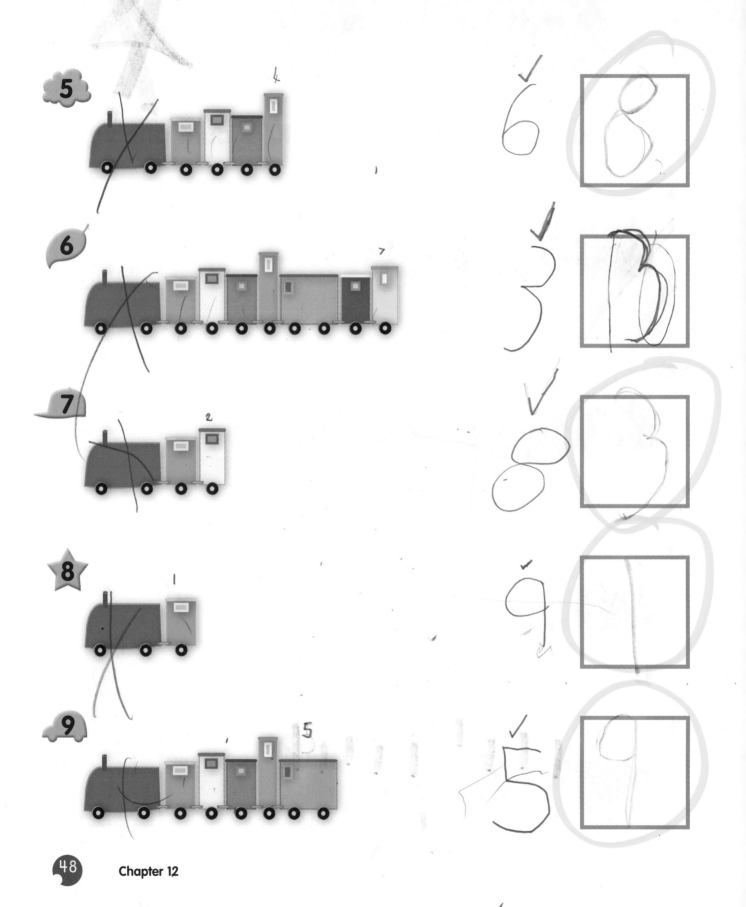

5

6

7

8

9

Color, count, and write.

1

There are 10 and .

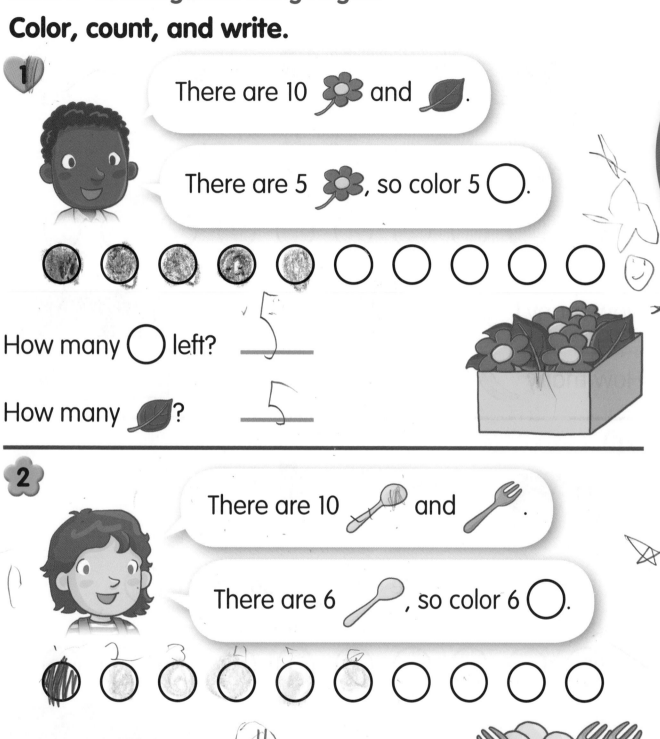

There are 5 , so color 5 ○.

○ ○ ○ ○ ○ ○ ○ ○ ○ ○

How many ○ left? 5

How many ? 5

2

There are 10 and .

There are 6 , so color 6 ○.

○ ○ ○ ○ ○ ○ ○ ○ ○ ○

How many ○ left? 4

How many ? 4

Color, count, and write.

3

There are 10 and .

There are 3 , so color 3 .

How many left? ____

How many ? ____

4

There are 10 and .

There are 8 , so color 8 .

How many left? ____

How many ? ____

Lesson 3 **Finding Differences Using Fingers**

Count, write, and circle.

1

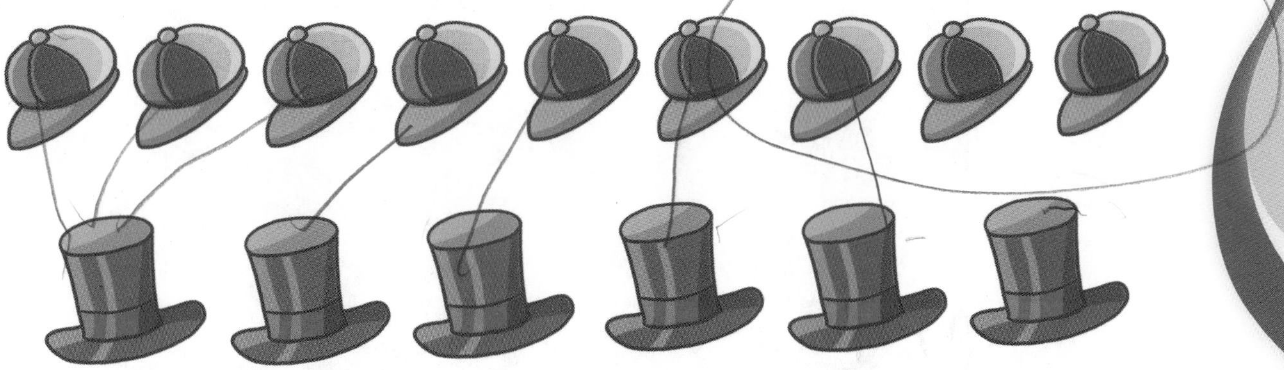

How many ? 9

How many ? 6

Are there more  or ?

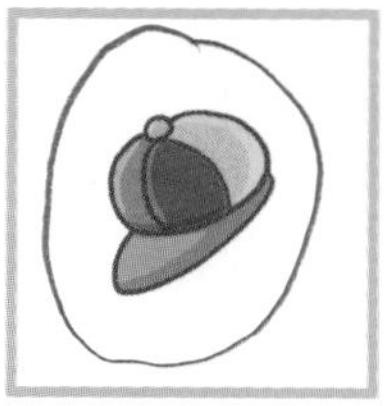 

How many more? 3

Are there fewer  or ?

How many fewer? 3

Count, write, and circle.

2

How many ? 4

How many 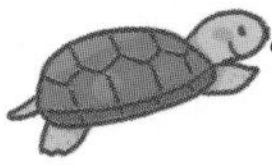? 8

Are there more  or 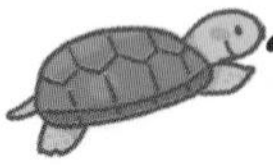?  

How many more? 4

Are there fewer  or 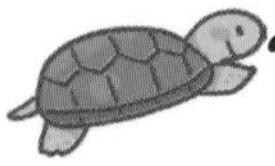?  

How many fewer? 4

Chapter 13 Patterns

Lesson 1 Repeating Patterns

The objects follow a repeating pattern. Circle the object that comes next.

1

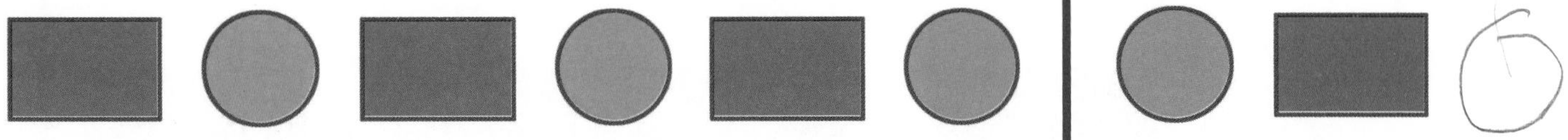

2

3

The shapes follow a repeating pattern.
Draw the missing shapes to complete the pattern.

1

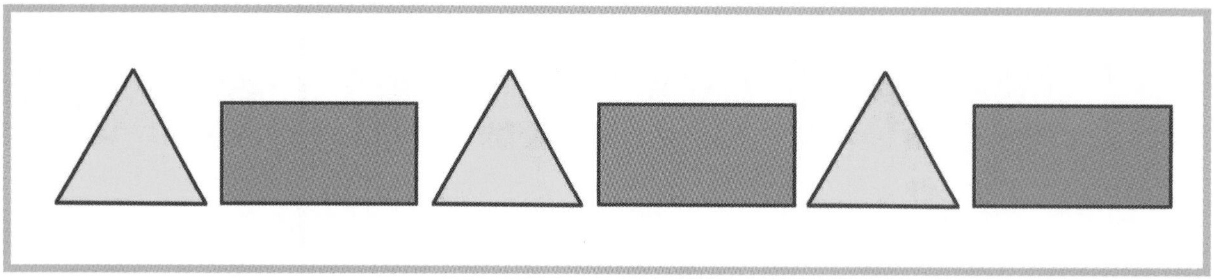

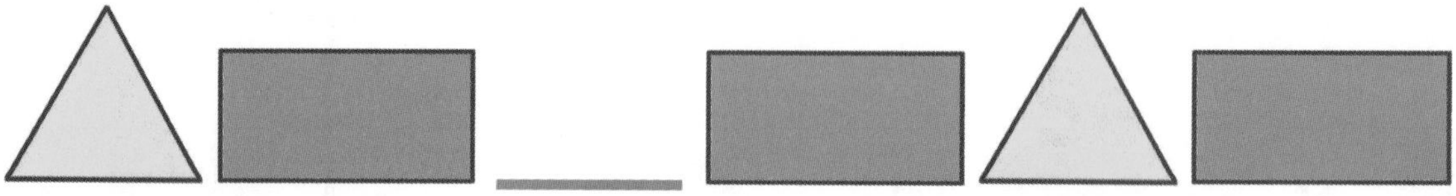

2

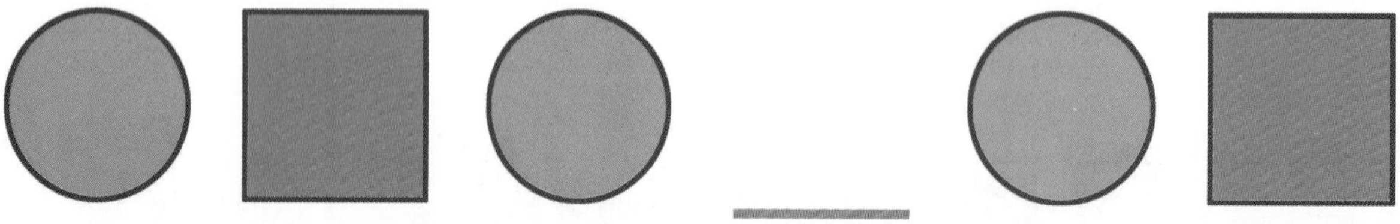

3

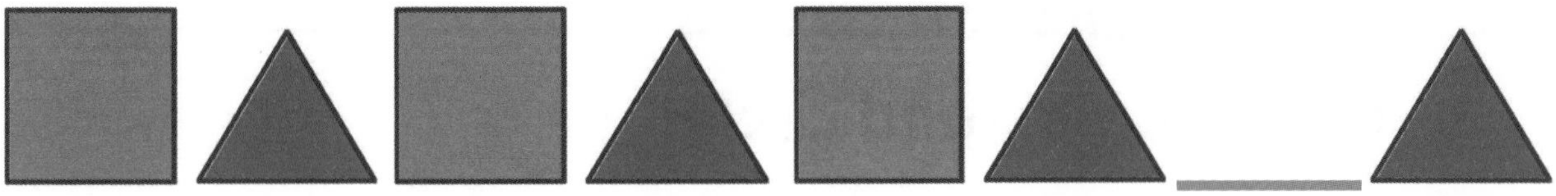

4

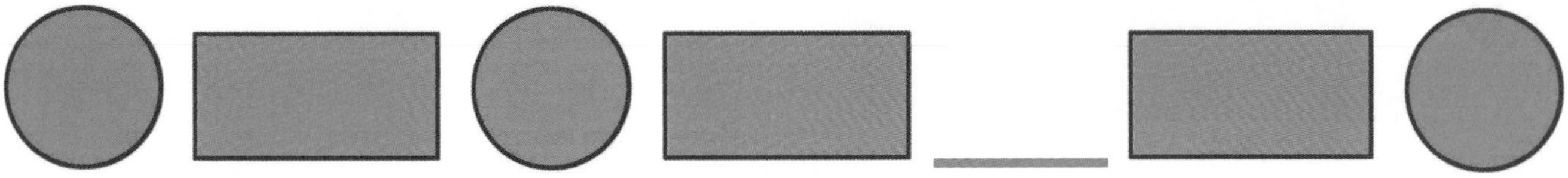

5

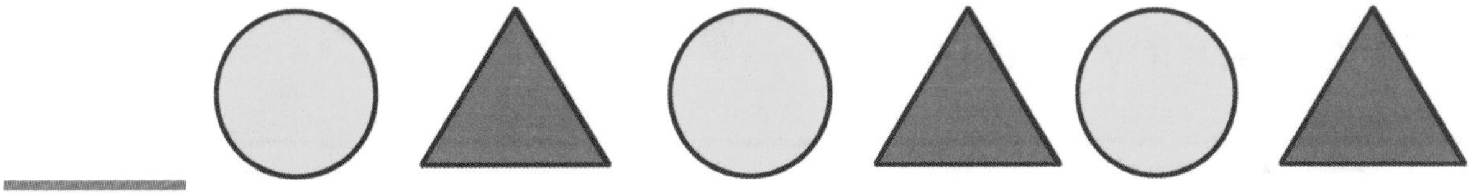

6

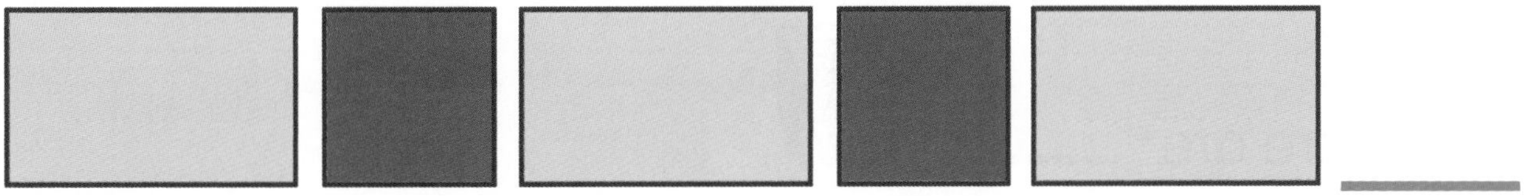

Chapter 14

Number Facts

Lesson 1 Number Facts to 10

Count, write, and circle.

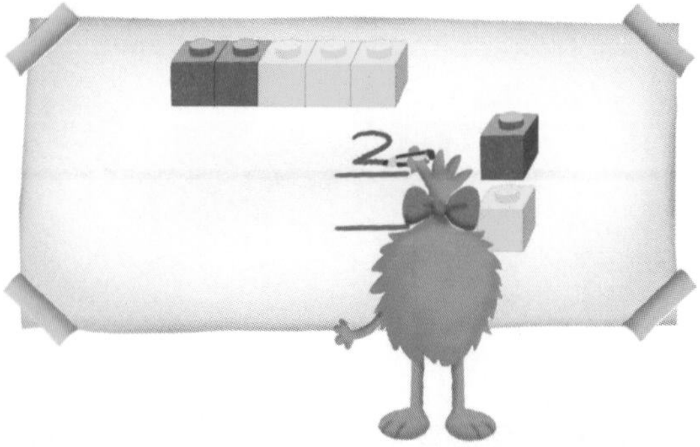

1 

There are 4 .

There are 2 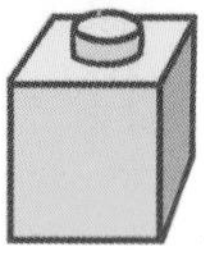.

How many in all? 2 4 (6)

---

2 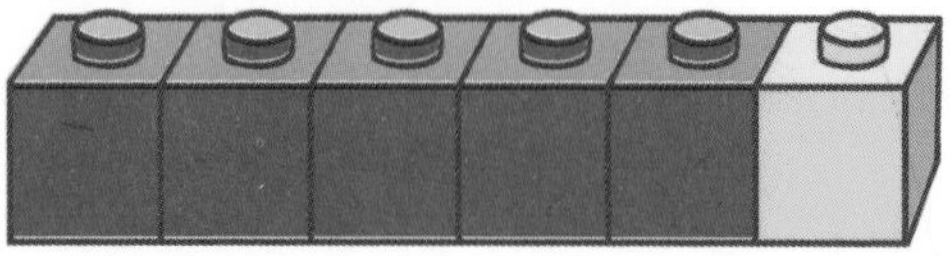

There are 5 .

There are 1 .

How many in all? 3 (6) 7

3

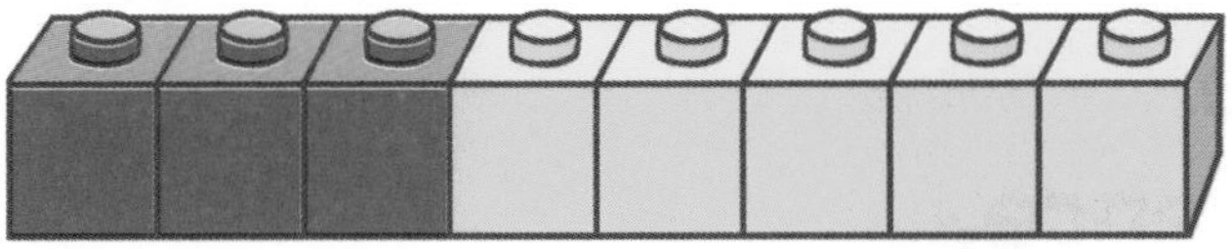

There are 3 .

There are 5 .

How many in all? (8) 9 10

4

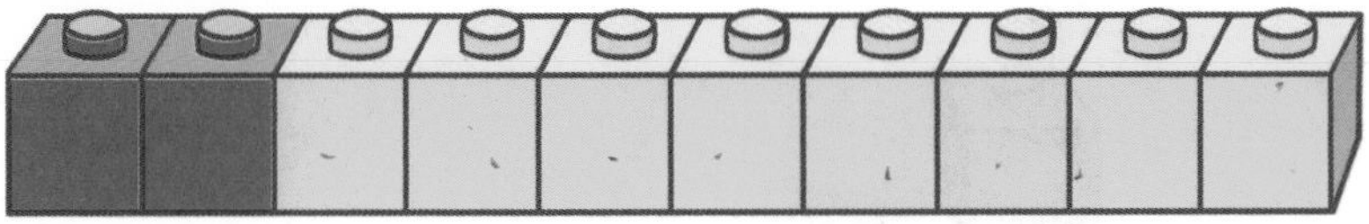

There are 2 .

There are 8 .

How many in all? 7 8 (10)

5

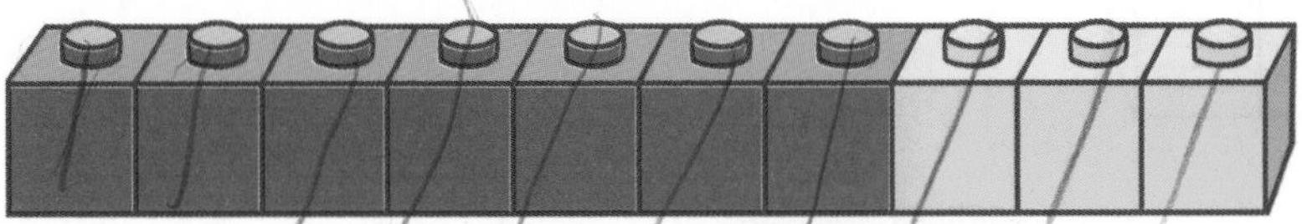

There are 7 .

There are 3 .

How many in all? (10) 11 12

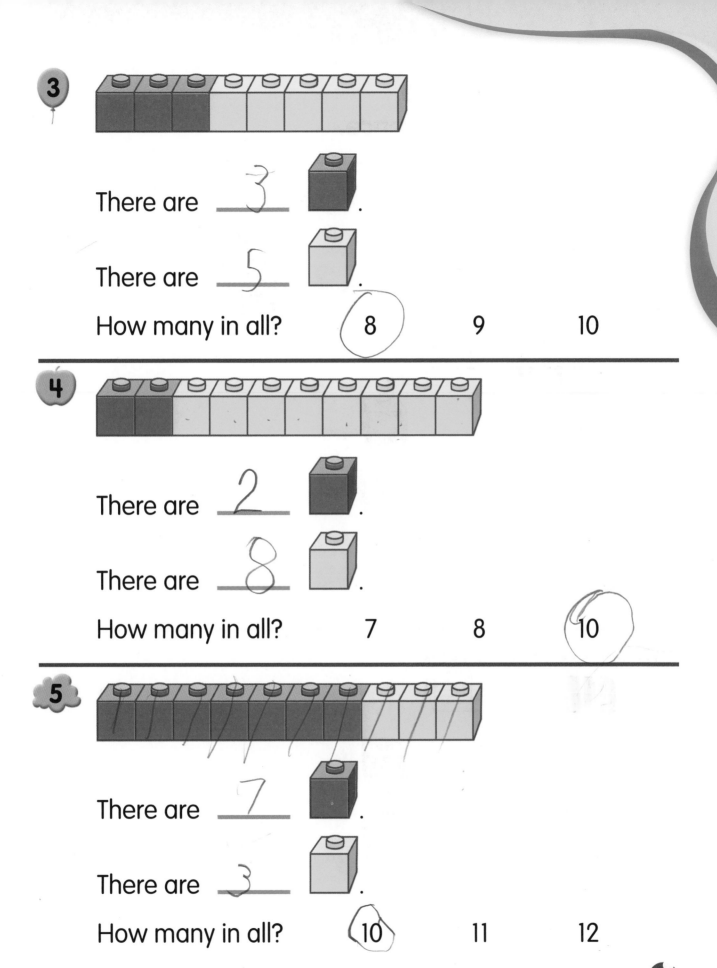

Color, count, and write.
Write the number sentence.

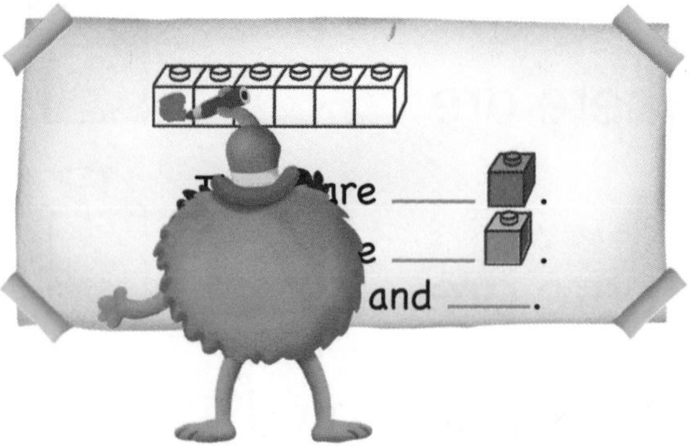

1

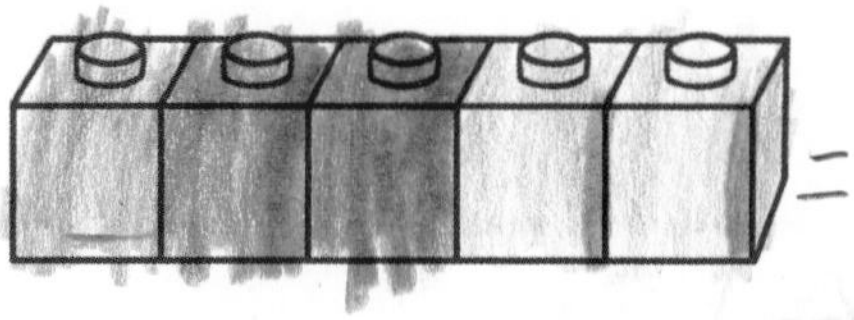

There are 3 .

There are 2 .

5 is 3 and 2 = 5.

2

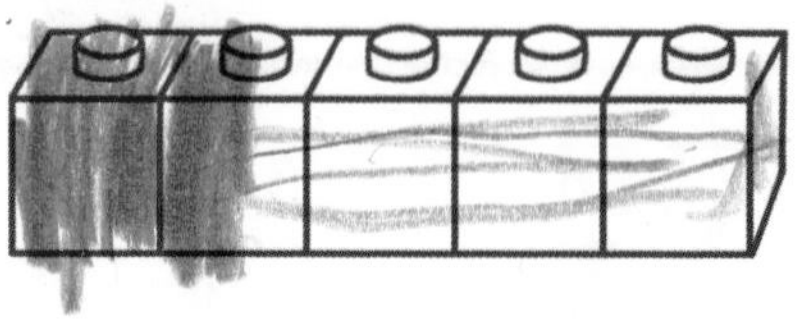

There are 1 .

There are 4 .

5 is 1 and 4 = 5.

3

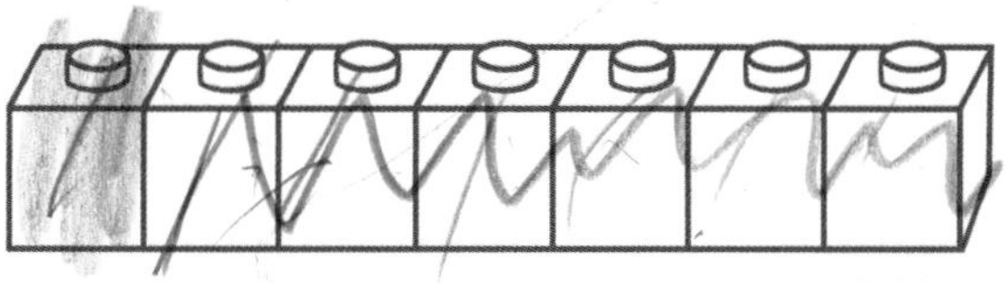

There are 6 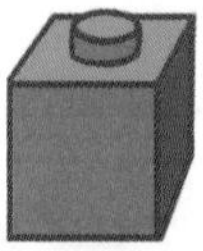.

There are 1 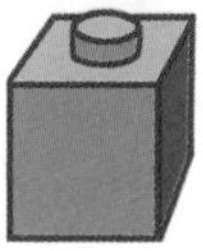.

7 is 6 and 1.

4

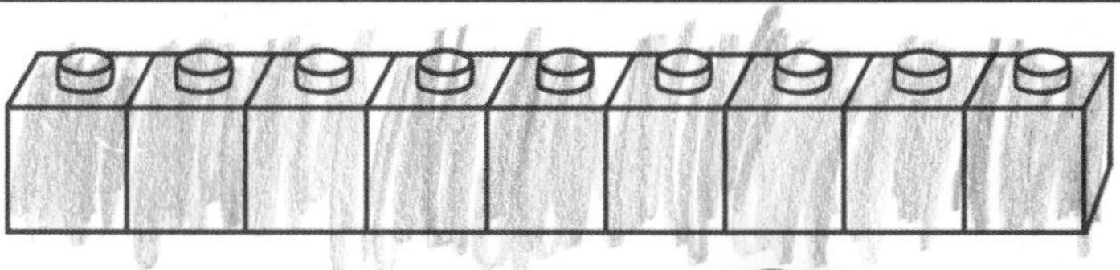

There are 8 .

There are 1 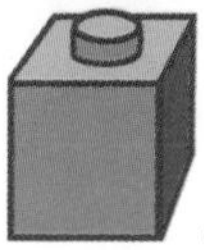.

9 is 8 and 1 = 9.

5

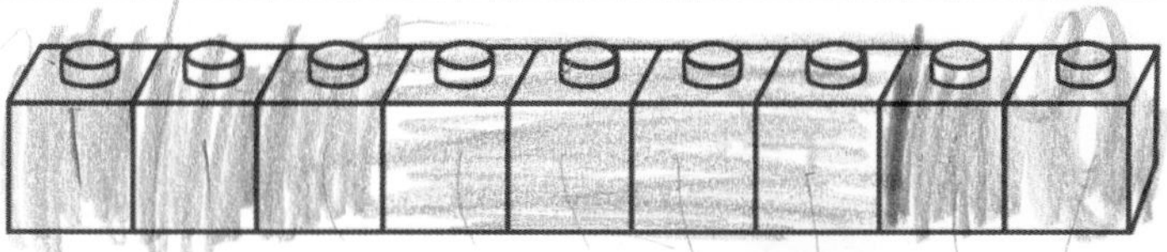

There are 7 .

There are 2 .

9 is 7 and 2 = 9.

Lesson 2 Combining Sets

Count and write.

1

Count how many. 9

How many more to make 10? 1

2

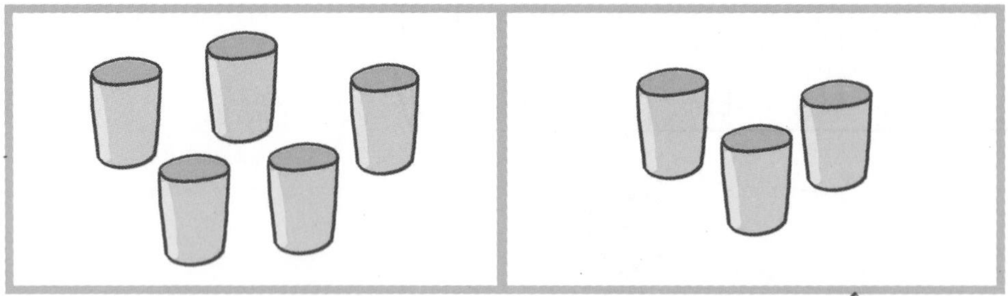

Count how many. 8

How many more to make 10? 2

3

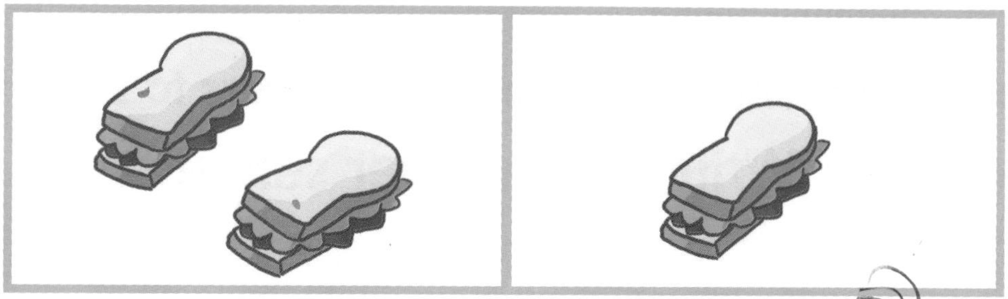

Count how many. 3

How many more to make 10? 7

4

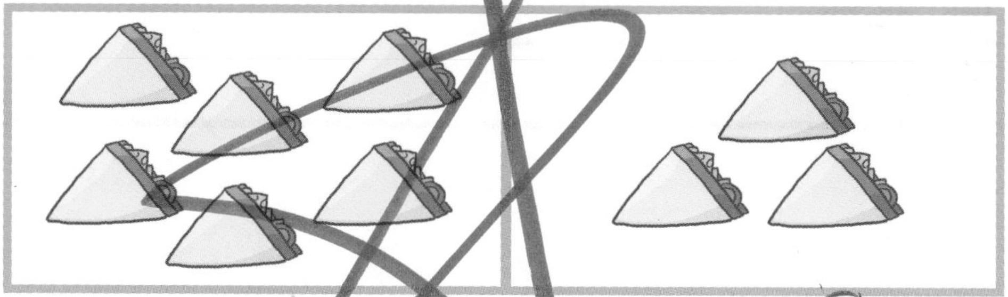

Count how many. 9

How many more to make 10? 1

5

Count how many. 5

How many more to make 10? 5

Lesson 3 **Composing and Decomposing Numbers to 20**

Count and write. Write the number sentence.

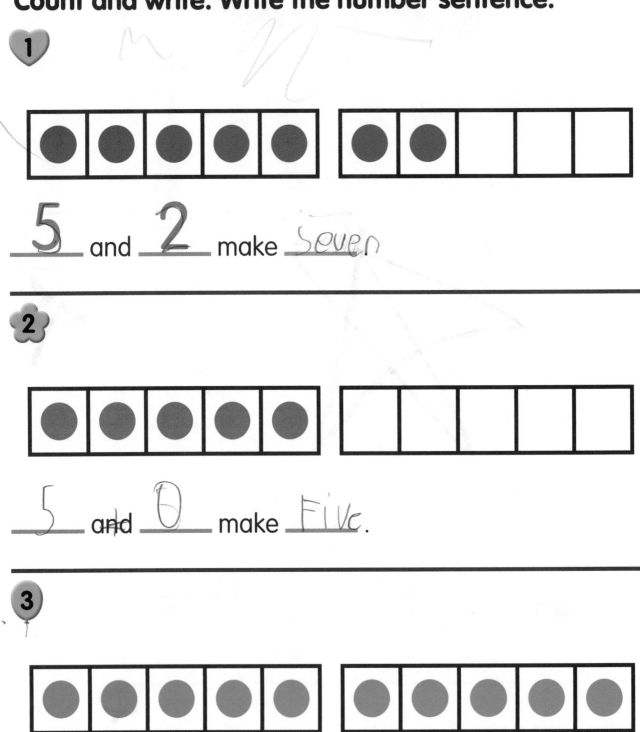

1

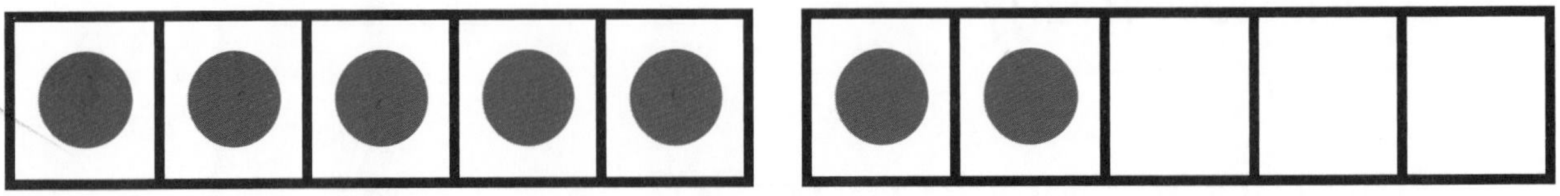

5 and 2 make seven.

2

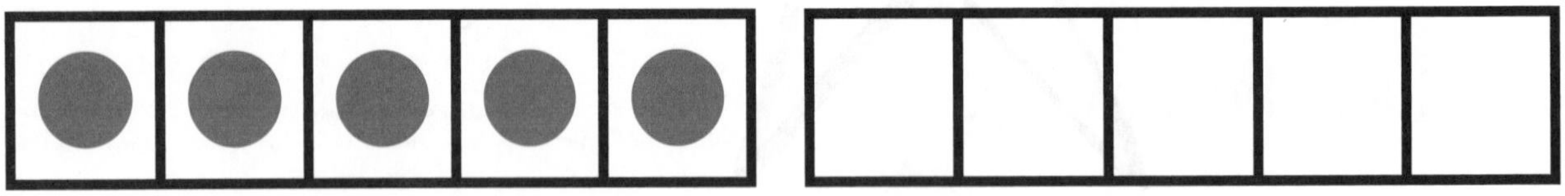

5 and 0 make Five.

3

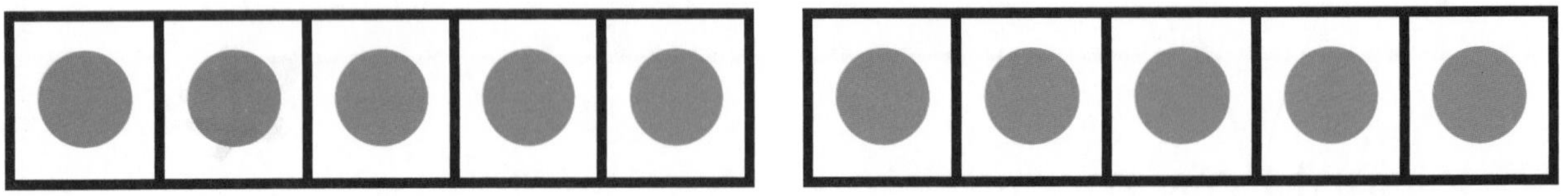

5 and 5 make ten.

4

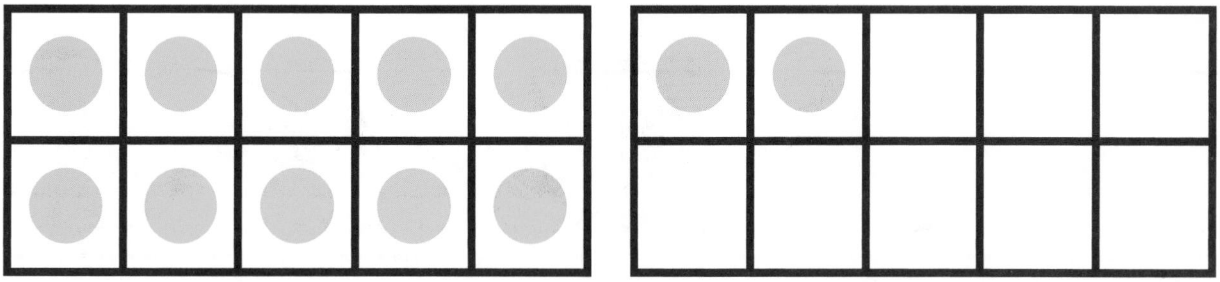

10 and 2 make twelve.

5

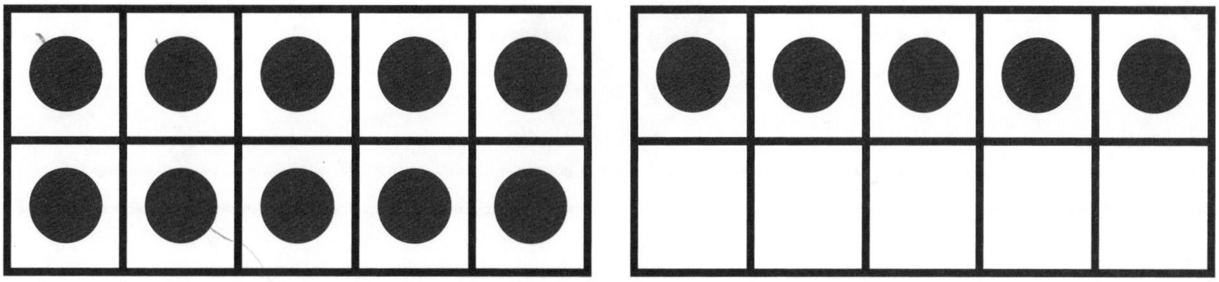

10 and 5 make fifteen.

6

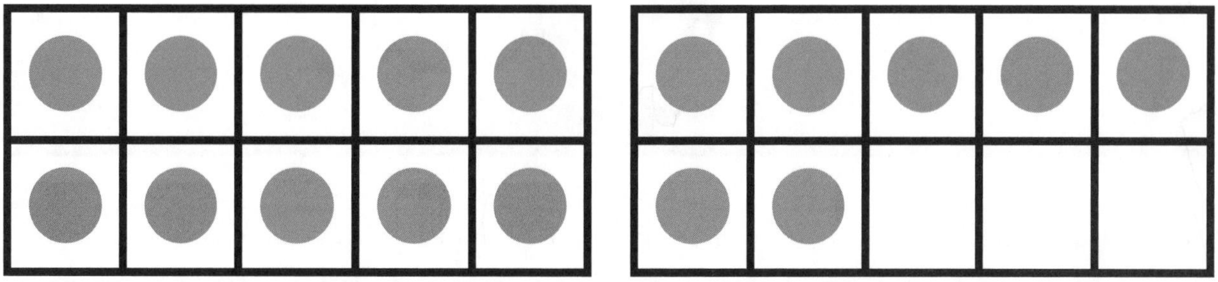

10 and 7 make seventeen.

Draw ◯. Write the number sentence.

1

7 is five and two.

2

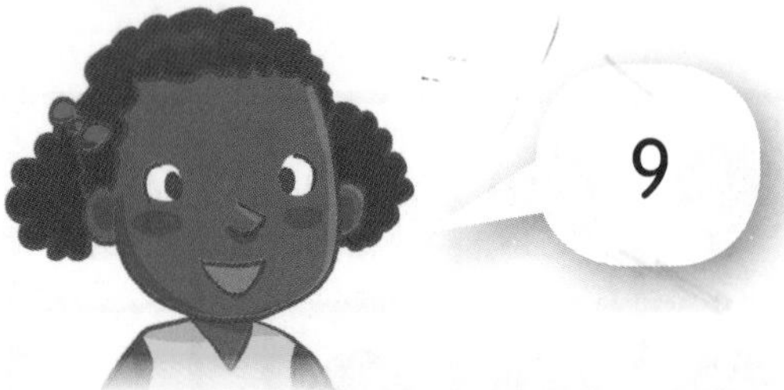

nine is five and four.

3

five is two and three.

4

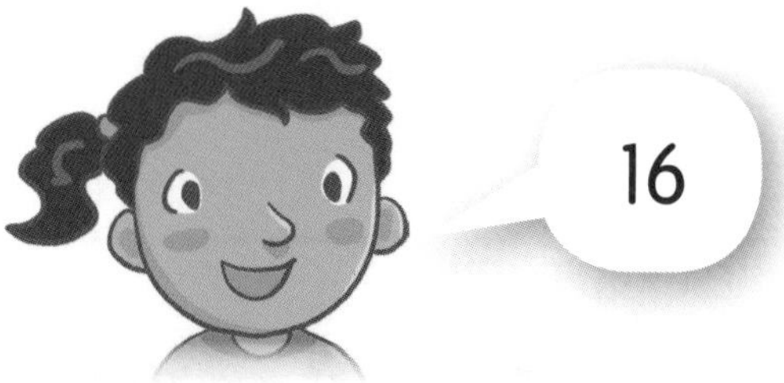

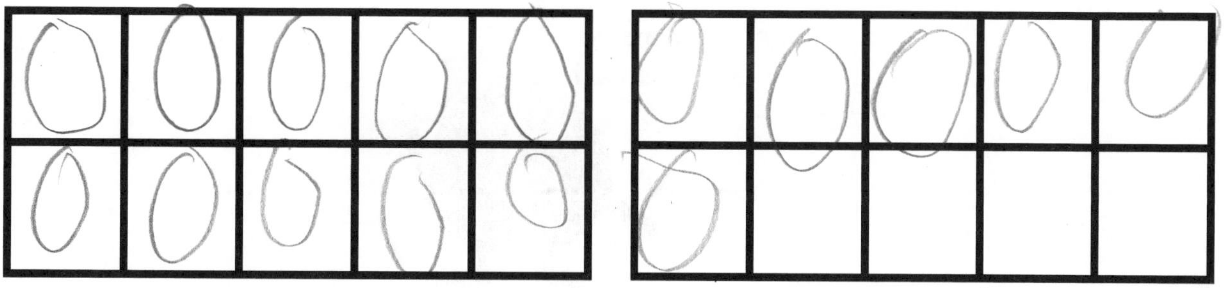

ixteen is ten and six.

5

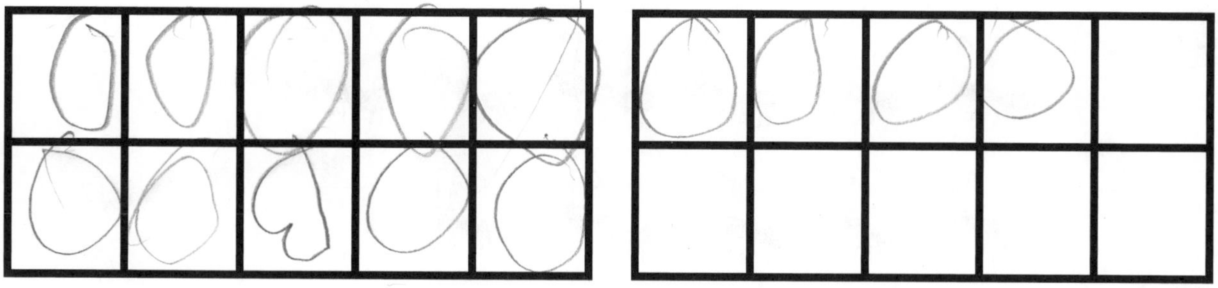

fourree is ten and four.

Lesson 4 Counting On

Count and write.

1

Count how many. 6

How many more to make 15? 9

2

Count how many. 11

How many more to make 15? 4

3

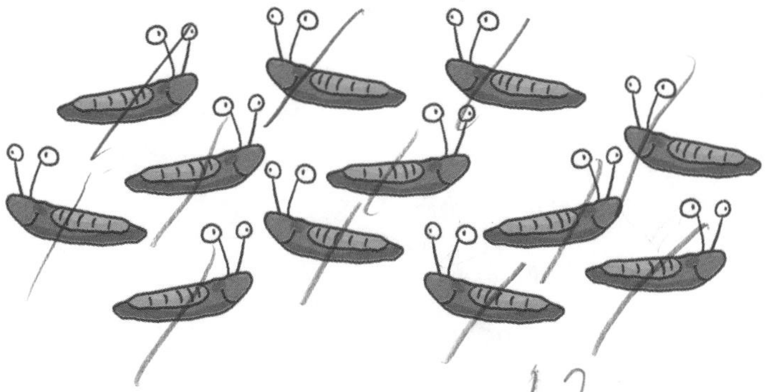

Count how many. 12

How many more to make 15? 3

4

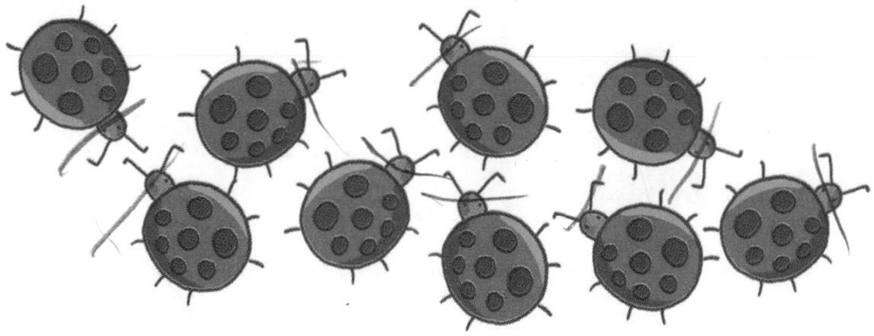

Count how many. 9

How many more to make 15? 6

5

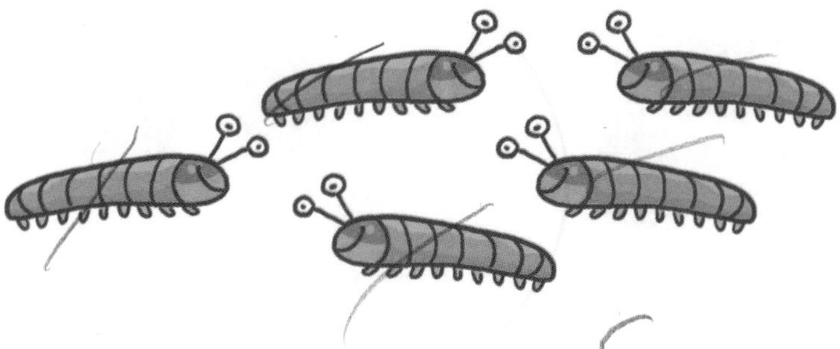

Count how many. 5

How many more to make 15? 10

Count and write.

1

Count how many. 8

How many more to make 15? 7

2

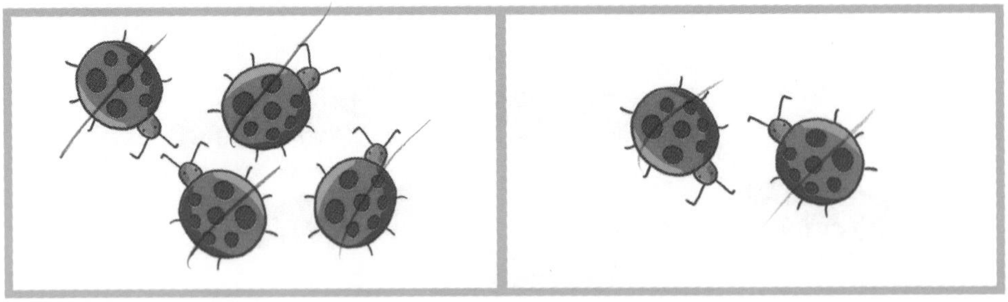

Count how many. 6

How many more to make 15? 9

3

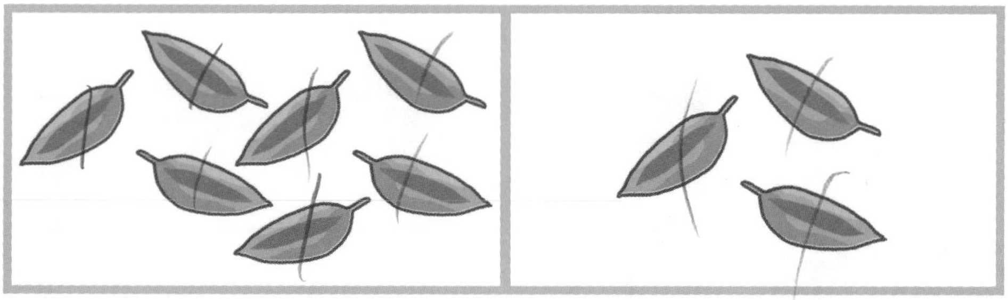

Count how many. 10

How many more to make 15? 5

4

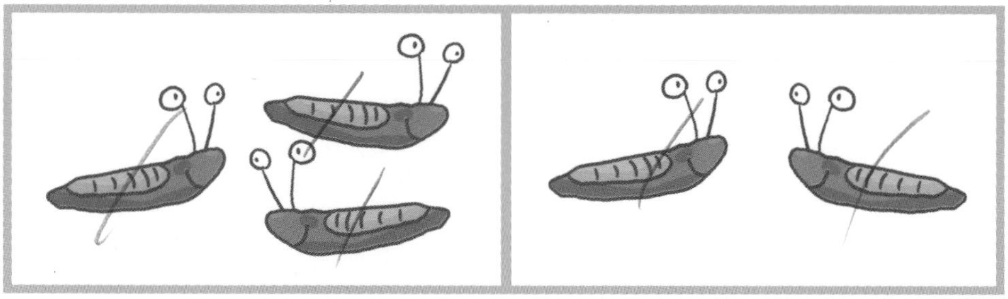

Count how many. 5

How many more to make 15? 10

5

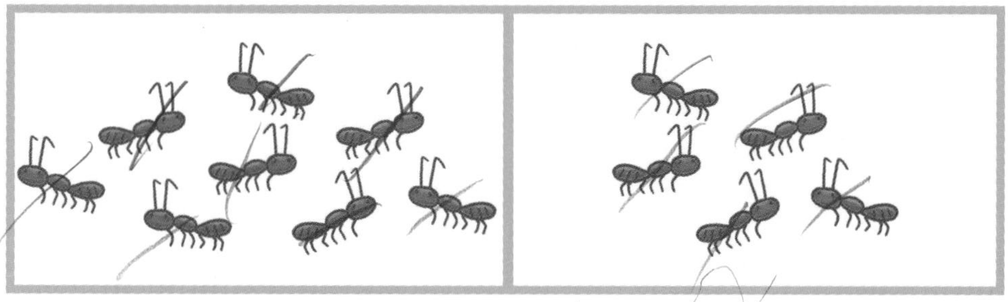

Count how many. 13

How many more to make 15? 2

Workmat 1

WORK MAT

Eshanaa